Gone
for the Day

Gone

FOR THE

Day

Family Fun in Central Texas

by

DEBORAH DOUGLAS

TEXAS A&M UNIVERSITY PRESS
College Station

Library of Congress Cataloging-in-Publication Data

Douglas, Deborah, 1952–
    Gone for the day : family fun in central Texas / by Deborah
Douglas. – 1st ed.
        p.   cm.
    Includes bibliographical references and index.
    ISBN 0-89096-650-8 (alk. paper)
    1. Texas—Tours. 2. Family recreation—Texas—Guidebooks.
3. Automobile travel—Texas—Guidebooks.   I. Title.
F384.3.D68   1995
917.6404'63—dc20   95-16181
                                                                  CIP

To all my families

Contents

Illustrations

Preface

We raise our children in capsules bounded by the streets between home, school, church, and the video rental store. Lurches from our capsule are billed as vacations—endpoints reached by airplane or after grueling and dueling hours in the family car. Preparing for conventional vacations—my husband claims they should be called trips because they are not vacations—is a strenuous task. So strenuous is it that you, in fact, need a vacation by the time you embark.

This book expands the capsule by introducing families to places and activities in the South Central Texas area. By definition, these adventures are completed in one day, thereby circumventing elaborate preparations.

Each section is about a place where a family can go "do something." It includes maps, snapshots, reservation information, phone numbers, and area interests. Excerpts from songs by Texas songwriters serve as epigraphs. In most sections, a cafe or restaurant is mentioned. Dollar signs follow each of the restaurant entries and designate relative price ranges, with $ being least expensive and $$$$ most expensive.

All in all, though, this is not the usual type of travel book. The trips we took were not subsidized. This means that I was under no obligation to say nice things about a place. These are places where my kids had fun. I would feel awful if, on my account, a family wasted a precious Saturday at a cruddy place. I have left the cruddy places in my pencil.

The information in this book is as accurate as possible; however, I have come to know that absolutely, positively sure is a relative term. For that reason, if it makes sense to do so, I suggest making a confirmatory phone call before you pile in the car, buckle your seatbelts, and reach escape velocity.

On their own level, day vacations are as great a challenge as conventional ones. It is difficult enough to gather a family for a meal, much less for an outing. You may encounter resistance from your children when you suggest that the family spend the day together. The animal magnetism of the Muppet Babies cartoons and the call of the mall are hard to ignore. And parents can always justify staying home.

To that, I say this: If you postpone vacations until all the yard work and housework are done, and the ironing basket is empty, and the desk is clean, your children will be grown. Only hollow memories of doing housework and yard work and watching cartoons will remain. I urge you to make other memories. You are entitled to them.

Acknowledgments

I would like to thank the following people for their help in preparation of this book.

First and foremost, I would like to thank my husband Andy, unofficial editor and best friend, for his unwavering support of this cockamamy idea of mine to write a book. Second and "foremore," I give credit to my daughter Jessica and son Andrew for being tough and candid critics of the day vacations—if an adventure has not passed muster with them, it isn't included in this book.

My parents Lorene and Ernest Denney and my younger sisters Teresa Denney, Pamela Denney Nielson, and Leisa Denney Taylor gave matter-of-fact support—it simply never occurred to any of them that I couldn't write a book if I decided to.

Three other families also saw me through to the end: my church family at Laurel Heights United Methodist Church, my professional family at Severance and Associates, and my friends in the Old Hippie Traveling Club, Scott and Barbara Lyford and Janie Kline.

Karen Courtney deserves mention for her cheerful but cold-hearted copyreading of the manuscript. That we made it through this project on excellent terms indicates the strength of our friendship.

I also want to thank my friend Priscilla Sowell, who taught me the difference between what is urgent and what is important and how to use a word processor, which is both.

I would like to thank Jim Behrens, Texas Parks and Wildlife guide, Kerrville regional office, for his assistance in providing information about the Old Tunnel bat colony and Paulyn Tree, a dispatcher with the Gillespie County sheriff's office, for researching the exact date of the disingenuous displacement of Balancing Rock. I would also like to thank Bill Botard, Gillespie County agricultural extension agent, for providing me with information about cow-calf pair grazing potential for improved and native range pastureland in the Central Texas area.

The following publishers have generously given permission to reprint lyrics from copyrighted works. All rights reserved. Used by permission. From "The Man with the Big Hat" by Steve Fromholz. © MCA Music Publishing Company (ASCAP). From "Listen to the Radio" by Nanci Griffith. © Irving Music, Inc. and Ponder Heart Music (BMI). From "Which Way Does That Old Pony Run" by Lyle Lovett. © Vector Management (ASCAP). From "What I Like about Texas" by Gary P. Nunn. © 1983 Guacamole Records/Gary P. Nunn. From "Crazy Wind" by James McMurtry. © 1989 Short Trip Music (BMI) Admin. by Bug. From "Northeast Texas Women" by Willis Alan Ramsey. © 1970 Wishbone Music (ASCAP). From "Gulf Coast Highway" by Nanci Griffith, James Brown, and Danny Flowers. © 1987 Danny Flowers Music (ASCAP) Admin. by Bug/Griffmill Music (BMI)/Rick Hall, Inc. (BMI). © 1987 Colgems-EMI Inc., Wing and Wheel Music, and Danny Flowers Music (ASCAP). International copyright secured. From "I Don't Love You Much Do I" by Guy Clark and Richard Leigh. © 1992 EMI April Music, Inc., GSC Music, and Lion-hearted Music. All rights controlled and administered by EMI April Music Inc. (ASCAP). International copyright secured. From "To Live Is to Fly" by Townes Van Zandt. © 1971 Columbine Music/Townes Van Zandt. From "Texas Cookin'" by Guy Clark. © 1976 Chappell and Co. From "Watermelon Dream" by Guy Clark. © 1988 EMI April Music Inc., and GSC Music. All rights controlled and administered by EMI April Music Inc. (ASCAP). International copyright secured. From "Boats to Build" by Guy Clark and Verlon Thompson. © 1992 EMI April Music Inc., GSC Music, and Ides of March Music. All rights controlled and administered by EMI April Music Inc. (ASCAP). International copyright secured. From "Mama's Cooking'" by Marcia Ball. © 1989 Rounder Records Corporation/ Marcia Ball. From "Jake's Song" by Steve Fromholz. © MCA Music Publishing Company (ASCAP). From "Vague Directions" by James McMurtry. © 1992 Short Trip Music (BMI) Admin. by Bug. From

"Silver Eagle Express" by Kinky Friedman. © 1973 by Ensign Music Corporation. From "Coming Home" by Roy Orbison, Will Jennings, and J. D. Souther. Published by Orbisongs, EMI Music and Blue Sky Rider. © 1986 EMI April Music Inc., Acuff Rose-Opryland Music and Blue Sky Rider. International copyright secured. From "Hometown Streets" by Nanci Griffith and James Hooker. © 1991 Irving Music, Inc. and Ponder Heart Music (BMI) and Rick Hall Music, Inc. (ASCAP).

Most of all, I want to thank all the friends and family members, especially my husband Andy and my brother-in-law Jamie Nielson, who make me laugh.

Last, I want to mention John Graves. He is my favorite writer. My ulterior motive for doing this book was to somehow finagle a way to meet this great man of Texas letters. Maybe, just maybe, he'll let me come visit him and bring along a buttermilk pie.

*Gone
for the Day*

Bandera
Ki-yi-yippee at the Running R

*Now the highlines chase the highways
And the fences close the range.
And to see a workin' cowboy
Is a sight that's mighty strange.
A cowboy's life was lonely
And his lot was not the best.
But if it wasn't for the life he lived
There wouldn't be no West.*
—Steve Fromholz, "The Man with the Big Hat"

"They can't be serious," was my first reaction when I saw Bandera's welcome sign claiming to be the "Cowboy Capital of the World." I had read that Bandera (population 924) was once a gathering spot for cattle drives, but that was a hundred years ago. Since the 1930s, Bandera has cultivated a guest ranch industry that attracts visitors from all over the world. Still, though, I wondered if that certified it as the cowboy capital of the *world*.

On second thought, what right have I to challenge Bandera's claim. I have lived in Texas most of my life, and I can name only two cowboys—Tinker Elms and John G. Prude. Tinker Elms passed away in early November, 1992, and John G. Prude is over ninety years old. I know ranchers and cattlemen and rodeo champions and snuff dippers and country-western singers and a raft of people, like myself, who wear jeans and boots and drink longnecks and use funny words like raft. So, who am I to take issue with Bandera's byname. When it gets right down to the lick-log, maybe it is the cowboy capital of the entire world.

It is a Texan's duty to perpetuate the positive, harmless parts of

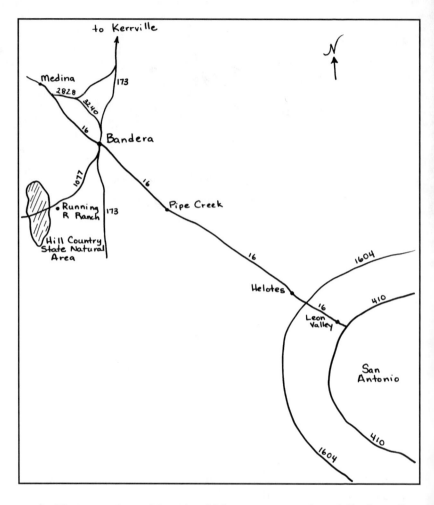

the Texas mystique. Men should lose money in the oil "bid'ness," wear string ties, and drive Suburbans. Women should make good buttermilk biscuits, be able to change a tire, and aspire to be governor. Everybody should love chicken-fried steak, ride horses, and support the team. If you are shirking your responsibility, a stable near Bandera offers you the chance to redeem yourself.

The **Running R Ranch** is 11 miles south of Bandera on FM Road 1077. Unlike other area guest ranches that give horseback riding priority to their overnight visitors or do not even accept day riders, the Running R Ranch deals mainly with day riders. Jo Cubbison and Charles "Doo" Robbins, partners at the Running R Ranch, can arrange guided horseback rides for one, two, or three hours, one-half day with lunch at the ranch or all day with lunch and a cookout supper at the ranch. They also offer one-hour breakfast rides and one-hour sunset rides, the latter with a wiener roast at a scenic spot.

Adult prices vary with the length of the ride, while children (six-to twelve-years old) ride at a flat fee of about $12 per hour per child. A two-hour ride for a family of four is about $100. Riders must be at least six years old and weigh less than 225 pounds.

On Tuesdays and Wednesdays, only one-hour rides are scheduled. All-day rides and breakfast rides are for groups of six or more. The phone number at the Running R Ranch is (210) 796-3984.

The Running R Ranch adjoins the **Hill Country State Natural Area,** which is one of the few state parks that permits horseback riding. Opened to the public in 1984, this 5,381-acre park has 32 miles of multi-use trails (horseback riding, all-terrain bicycling, and hiking). In fact, horseback riders are the park's most frequent visitors. A sign near the park superintendent's office shows who yields to whom: hikers yield to horseback riders, cyclists yield to horseback riders and hikers, and horseback riders have total right of way.

The developed trails in the Hill Country State Natural Area lead through various Hill Country terrains: savannah grasslands, limestone escarpments, and seasonal creek bottoms. Some trails lead to hilltops with towering (and radio towerless) views of fine Texas Hill Country.

Except for Tuesdays and Wednesdays, when the park is closed, all guided horseback rides from the Running R Ranch follow trails in the Hill Country State Natural Area. The course of the rides varies from day to day to minimize the negative impact of the "sacrifice area," as Barton Warnock, Professor Emeritus at Sul Ross University, calls a trail created for human (and horse) use.

As of September, 1992, the Running R Ranch and the Hill Country State Natural Area have teamed up to sponsor monthly interpretive horseback rides. Holders of the Texas Conservation Passport (see Appendix 1) are eligible to register. These guided rides are popular and are booked months in advance of the ride dates. Holders of the Texas Conservation Passport can also participate in the Hill Country State Natural Area interpretive hikes, which are conducted at

Horseback riders at Hill Country State Natural Area

9 A.M. on some Sundays. For topics and reservations, contact park superintendent Shaun Heavey at (210) 796-4413.

It was during one of these interpretive hikes that I learned about ball moss (*Tillandsia recurvata*). Ball moss is gray, tufty stuff that grows around tree limbs. In some instances it transforms the lower, sun-deprived limbs into woolly, wooden blobs. The limbs eventually droop and break off but, I am told, not because of the ball moss.

Ball moss supposedly doesn't hurt the tree. It also doesn't hurt the telephone wires that it encircles. It is an epiphyte and derives its nutrients from the air. If a tree or group of oak trees are dead or dying, their condition is more likely due to oak decline or oak wilt (*Ceratocystis fagacearum*), a beetle-born fungus. This disease ravages entire mottes of oak trees by insidiously spreading through the intertwining roots. Trenching techniques to disrupt root connections and fungicide injections to kill the bug have proven somewhat effective in local control of oak wilt; however, these measures are expensive.

AREA INTERESTS

Bandera Downs is a horse racetrack located 2 miles southeast of town on State Highway 16. The racing season runs from early March to late November, except for two weekends in August. Post time is 1 P.M. on Friday, Saturday, Sunday, and on Memorial Day and Labor Day. General admission for an unreserved bleacher seat is less than the price of a movie. Higher-priced seats are available in the smoke-free, air-conditioned Upper Jockey Club. Pari-mutuel wagering is vigorous, and a three-day take averages a million dollars. I would include more information, but I feel my Baptist-reared tongue cleaving to the roof of my mouth. Call (210) 796-7781.

Bandera Forge is located at 803 Main Street in Bandera, near the middle of town. Blacksmith Ken "Pee Wee" Stroud is happy to show onlookers his skill at forging custom-made branding irons. You can call him at (210) 796-7184. Open, according to Pee Wee, from "about seven in the morning until around eight at night."

Texas Hill Country Rocker is located at Bandera's main intersection at the corner of Highway 16 and Main Street. Their specialty is handcrafted western red cedar rocking chairs. As you drive by, a gigantic rocker in the side yard catches your attention. A little step

Bandera Forge

stool beside it allows ascent for the necessary photo. The regular-sized rocking chairs are good gifts, especially for people who like to sit on the porch and drink buttermilk. Call (210) 796-8109.

River Oak Inn Restaurant is located at 1105 Main in Ban-dera at the west end of town. Outside seating on a wooden deck overlooks a creek and a grassy field, which slopes down to the Medina River with its bald cypress sentinels. Dieters can order a chicken fajita salad. The rest of us can order seafood, steaks, Mexican food, and burgers. The restaurant is open every day between 10 A.M. and 2 P.M. and between 5 P.M. and 9 P.M. Call (210) 796-7751. $$

Flores Country Store in Helotes (population 1,606) is a family-oriented honky tonk. That sounds oxymoronic, or maybe just plain moronic, but it's not. With live country music, longneck beer and a sawdust dance floor, it is, in this part of Texas, the king of honky tonks. Flores Country Store is open on Friday from 5 P.M. to midnight, on Saturday from 3 P.M. to 1 A.M., and on Sunday from 3 P.M. to 10 P.M. A message on the answering machine tells you what's in store for the weekend; call (210) 695-8827.

Bastrop

Pine Needle Sliding at Bastrop State Park

My mama's gonna' call and say, "Where's she gone?"
He'll say, "Down the road with the radio on."
—Nanci Griffith, "Listen to the Radio"

Who says you can't go tobogganing in Texas? Pine needle sliding at Bastrop State Park, a mile east of Bastrop (population 4,235) on State Highway 21, is as much fun as sledding in Colorado and New Mexico. The trip requires less air travel—none actually—and is less expensive. Lift tickets are not required; however, you must pay a state park admission fee, unless you have a Texas Conservation Passport (see Appendix 1). Cardboard boxes, opened and trimmed to toboggan size, are the only necessary equipment. "Powder" is freshest on fall days, but any fairly dry day will do.

This is one of my children's favorite day trips. If you are disinclined to let your children have some old-fashioned fun, chop logic this way: This trip is environmentally sensitive. You are recycling cardboard, and while you are at it, you can recycle some old bread. The ducks at the park are helpful.

For pine needle sliding you need pine trees that shed pine needles. Most of the state's pine trees are in East Texas; however, Bastrop State Park is a 3,500-acre patch of East Texas loblolly pines conveniently located for the residents of South Central Texas. Since the main pine forest is 80 miles away, I guess you call it a branch forest, or, as my husband suggests, a shruburb. I try to avoid such distractive neologizing.

Like the bigtooth maples of Lost Maples State Natural Area, the loblolly pines of Bastrop State Park are survivors of the Pleistocene Ice Age when the weather was cooler and wetter. The sandy, acidic

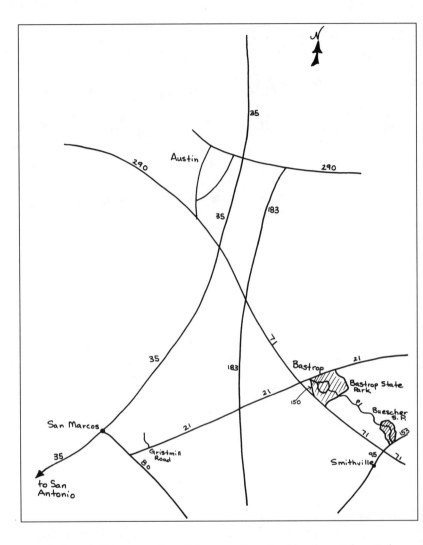

soil that pine trees need to thrive was deposited by the mighty Colorado River when it was mightier.

The sandy, acidic red dirt of Bastrop is the reason I wrote this book. For her 1991 school science fair project, my daughter tested the pH level of soils from all over Texas. She wanted to prove that soil alkalinity decreases from west to east (it does). We had intended to go to Big Thicket during the Christmas vacation to collect an East Texas soil sample, but my daughter got chicken pox. Being the long-suffering mother that I am, I left my scabby, crabby daughter with the baby-sitter, packed a thermos of hot coffee and some Steve Winwood tapes, and drove to Bastrop for some East Texas soil. I had fun and hatched the book idea to warrant more day trips. Reading books by Kinky Friedman lent me the audacity to carry it through. I figured if a curmudgeonly Texas singer could write a book, so could I.

The only complicated part of pine needle sliding is finding the one hill that all sliders agree is the very best hill. Numerous slopes suitable for pine needle sliding can be spotted from Park Road 1A, which originates at the park entrance at the convergence of State Highway 21 and Loop 150, just east of Bastrop. (A detailed map of the park showing Park Road 1A is available at park headquarters.) Park Road 1A makes a 3-mile circle through the park. It is quite narrow, so I suggest parking your car in one of the many provided spaces and walking to the "lift area."

Once the very best hill is found, the rest is easy: trudge to the top of the very best hill, sit or lie or stand on the cardboard toboggan, and slide down. Avoid slamming into a pine tree.

The cardboard toboggans can double as shields when the pine cone war starts. Pine cones are sharp. I went to work one Monday with a scuffed nose. The conversations with colleagues who were impolite enough to ask about it went something like this:

"What happened to your nose?"

"A pine cone."

"A what?"

"A pine cone. I got hit in the nose with a pine cone."

"How did that happen?"

"My son threw it at me."

"Good grief! That coulda' put your eye out."

"Naw, I had on sunglasses. I'm thinking about having the kids wear goggles when we're having a pine cone war, though."

"You mean, you threw pine cones at your children?"

"Oh, heck, yeah. I started the war."

A ten-acre pond is located at the northern curve of Park Road 1A. There are picnic tables and ducks to feed, but swimming is not allowed. If you want to go swimming, the park operates a freshwater **swimming pool** from Memorial Day to Labor Day. It is open every day except Tuesday and Wednesday from noon to 6:45 P.M. Lifeguards

Pine needle sliding, Bastrop State Park

are on duty. The admission fee is only a few dollars. It is the only public pool in Bastrop, so, like pools everywhere, it can get a bit crowded on hot summer afternoons. For more information about the Bastrop State Park swimming pool, call (512) 321-2101.

For the hardy, there is an 8-mile loop **hiking trail**. The trailhead and trailtail are located one-half mile apart on the eastern side of Park Road 1A. For the less robust, like me and my family, there is a shortcut that reduces the loop hike to 2 miles, or about one hour hiking time. I suggest you park at the lot near the southern trailhead, walk the one-half mile (slightly uphill) along Park Road 1A to the northern trailhead, and begin the Lost Pines Hiking Trail. Maps are available at park headquarters. There are no rest rooms or drinking water along the trail. It would be a good idea to take some water, especially during the warm months.

Take binoculars if you are interested in birds. Bastrop State Park is located in what naturalists call the Central Flyway. This region is the overlap area among bird species that are endemic to the eastern United States and prevalent in the western United States. More than two hundred species of birds have been seen in the park, including pileated and red-headed woodpeckers. A bird checklist is available at park headquarters.

The hiking trail is strewn with pine needles, which muffle your steps and allow you to eavesdrop on the breeze blowing through the pine trees and hardwoods. It is best to stay on the trail, since poison ivy and poison oak, with their telltale three leaves, are part of the understory. Along the way is a small frog pond and a rock outcropping for a sit-and-rest-a-minute.

Bastrop State Park has 78 campsites, some with water only, some with water and electricity, and some with water, electricity, and sewage disposal. Camping is also allowed on the hiking trail. There are also 13 rustic stone cabins, a group campsite, group barracks, a dining hall for up to 90 people. The cabins, numbered 1 through 12 and 14 (no number 13), were built to last during the 1930s by recruits in the Civilian Conservation Corps (CCC).

The CCC was organized in 1933 as a public works program for the unemployed as part of President Franklin D. Roosevelt's New Deal. In 1935, during the harshest days of the Great Depression, nearly 20,000 men were working in CCC companies in Texas alone. The majority of these camps were forest and soil conservation camps, but about 5000 men were assigned to park development.

In 1942, when Congress ended the CCC, Texas had fifty-six parks to show for these men's efforts. (Other parks mentioned in this book with a CCC history are Inks Lake, Longhorn Caverns, Kerrville, Blanco, Buescher, Palmetto, and Goliad.)

The construction of buildings and recreation improvements followed standards set by the National Park Service, which meant that park buildings should be "sensitive to the natural surroundings" and "relate closely to their sites." This style of architecture has come to be known as NPS Rustic. Built from Bastrop County stone and wood, the cabins and refectory at Bastrop State Park embrace the NPS ideal that buildings should look like they belong where they are. The cabins, located on the shores of the lake, really do look like they emerge from the ground.

For fee schedule and reservations for the campsites, group camp, and the cabins, call (512) 389-8900 (See Appendix 1). For other information about the park, write Park Superintendent, Bastrop State Park, Box 518, Bastrop, Texas 78602, or call (512) 321-2101.

In addition to pine needle sliding, swimming, hiking, camping, and feeding ducks, you can also play golf at Bastrop State Park. The **Lost Pines Golf Course** is operated by the Lost Pines Golf Association. The nine-hole golf course is open year round. To hit a practice bucket on the driving range, rent a cart, rent clubs, and play a round costs about $25. For prices and to reserve a tee time, call (512) 321-2327.

AREA INTERESTS

Buescher State Park is the smaller, less piney, more post-oaky sister of Bastrop State Park. Its main draws are a scenic fishing lake and less crowded campsites. It is umbilicated to Bastrop State Park by 11 miles of narrow, winding, pine needle–strewn ribbon of asphalt named Park Road 1C. (The signs say 13 miles, but it is really only 11 and a pleasant drive, at that.) Buescher State Park can also be reached via State Highway 71. For more information call (512) 237-2241, or write the Park Superintendent, P.O. Box 75, Smithville, Texas 78957.

Lock Drug at 1003 Main Street in Bastrop is owned by David Lock, a native of Bastrop and also its mayor. After attending pharmacy school and working a few years for a retail pharmacy chain, Mr. Lock returned to Bastrop in 1970 and bought the drugstore. The building was recorded as an official Texas historical landmark in 1968 and as a national historic site in 1978. A plaque out front explains why. Children couldn't care less about the building's history, but they might be interested in the soda fountain, complete with ice cream and frozen yogurt. Lock Drug is open Monday through Friday, 9:45 A.M. to 6 P.M. (fountain closes at 5 P.M.), and Saturday, 9:45 A.M. to 5 P.M. It is closed on Sunday. Call (512) 321-2422.

Fisherman's Park (also called Riverfront Park) is at the corner of

Lock Drug, Bastrop

Farm Street and Wilson Drive, three blocks west of Main Street on the Colorado River. It is a city park funded by the Texas Parks and Wildlife Department and the Lower Colorado River Authority. It has a boat and tube launch area, sports fields, tennis courts, picnic tables and grills, portable toilets, and a fenced playscape overlooking the river. The park hours are 6 A.M. to 10 P.M. There is no admission fee.

Texas Grill Restaurant is mixed in with the fast-food restaurants and gas stations on Highway 71, just west of the Colorado River bridge. It is open twenty-four hours a day, seven days a week, with a cafeteria line open 11 A.M. to 2 P.M. every day. Menu items include steaks, seafood, chicken-fried steak, fried chicken, Mexican food, sandwiches, and for Aunt Leisa, the dieter, chef salad and taco salad. The children's menu has Tommy Tucker (fried chicken drumstick), Jack and Jill (ground beef patty or chicken-fried steak, potatoes, and salad), and Humpty Dumpty (scrambled eggs and bacon). Among the beverages is buttermilk. It is located in Bastrop at 101 Highway 71 West. Call (512) 321-5491. $$

Eugene Schnautz Family Gristmill is located less than a mile off State Highway 21 on Gristmill Road (Hays County Road 153), 9.5 miles from the Interstate Highway 35 turnoff to go to Bastrop. Behind a peeling painted door, marked with the words "Self Service Gristmill Room," is a freezer with five-pound sacks of stone-ground cornmeal and wheat flour. Recipes for cornbread and whole wheat bread are printed on the sides of the sacks. If you care to buy something, leave your money ($1.25 per sack) in the red plastic coffer and record your purchase in the spiral notebook. I asked Mr. Schnautz if he had ever had a problem with theft. He said that workers had borrowed money a few times, but, so far, he hadn't come up short at the end of the week. He has owned the gristmill since 1978. He reminded me to put my cornmeal in the refrigerator, since he adds no preservatives. His mailing address is Route 1, Box 79D, Kyle, Texas 78640. Call (512) 398-2593 for more information.

Boerne
Exploring a Cave without a Name

But what's riches to you
Just ain't riches to me.
—Lyle Lovett, "Which Way Does That Old Pony Run"

Cave without a Name (so named because it was considered too pretty to name) is also a cave without a billboard or a brochure or a busload of tourists. There are several superb show caverns in the Hill Country, but in my family's opinion, this unadvertised cavern near Boerne (population 4,476) "whups the tar" out of the others. Those aren't the exact words of my children. At least, I hope they're not that colloquial when they are describing nature's beauty.

The cave is open every day except Tuesday from 9:45 a.m. to 4:30 p.m. Reservations are not required, but a phone call ([210] 537-4212) to tour guide and resident troglophile, Eugene Ebell, would be polite. Admission for a family of four is about half the price of a single ticket to a theme park. The guided tour takes about one hour. Wear comfortable walking shoes, and bring plenty of film since neither are for sale at the gift shop.

To reach Cave without a Name, head north from Boerne on State Highway 474 for 5 miles. Turn right (northeast) on Kreutzberg Road, and follow the signs, some peeling and unpromising, to the end of the dirt road. On the right sits a brown trailer house. Knock on the door. Either Mr. Ebell will answer the door or his wife will call, "He's down at the cave." If the latter is the case, follow the path for fifty yards to an unimpressive two-room limestone building. This is the hospitality and registration area. Mr. Ebell will either be waiting (for sure, if you called ahead) or will have left a message on the chalkboard telling you when he'll be back up to ground level.

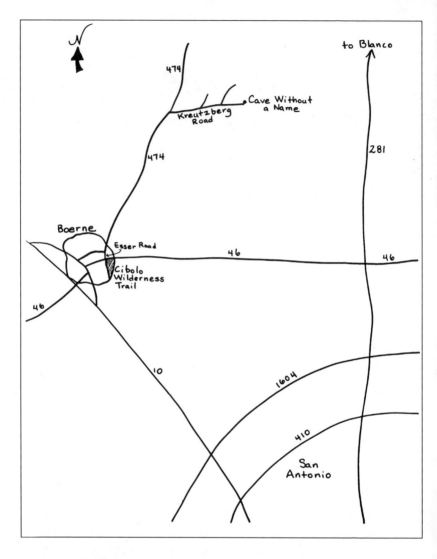

Mr. Ebell does not apologize for the modest surface structures. On the contrary, he is a bit reproachful when he points out the commercialism of other show caves. Who needs curio shops and popcorn stands when solid and quiet beauty lies ninety feet below the surface of the Edwards Plateau?

Rock and concrete steps lead down to a gigantic cavern partially divided into rooms by stalactites, stalagmites, and columns. As you follow Mr. Ebell along the flat, gravel paths, he points out formations with names like Orange Sherbet, Queen's Crown, Fishing Pole, and Christmas Tree. He shows you formations that look like a dolphin, a bear, a monkey, an eagle, an ice cream cone, marshmallows, and a cluster of grapes. He is proudest of the limestone curtains with alternating white and brown streaks that look like huge slabs of bacon. There is even a limestone nativity scene, complete with a shepherd and wise men, formed millions of years before the actual event—now, that is a master plan.

The Edwards Plateau is riddled with underground caverns. These

Grape clusters, Cave without a Name, Boerne

Cibolo Creek Trail, Cibolo Wilderness Trail

were formed when rainwater seeped into fractures in the limestone. The natural acidity of the rainwater slowly dissolved the walls of the fractures and formed underground channels. As the water table lowered with the down cutting of streams and rivers, the upper caves slowly drained, leaving the passageways relatively dry; however, these passageways were not totally dry. Rainwater continued to pass through these caverns, depositing tiny bits of limestone in their headlong trickle toward the water table. Dripstone formations (stalagmites, stalactites, and the columns that are formed when the two meet mid-cave) are the creation of this phase of the water cycle.

Cave without a Name is 80 percent active. Twelve hours after a good rain, the cave's surfaces are slippery and its quiet recesses amplify tiny splashes. The travertines, the most extensive in any Hill Country cavern, are brimming with cool, potable water. Travertines, or rim stones, are limestone deposits that form a honeycombed terrace of shallow pools.

The walls of the cavern are the exposed underside of the Glen Rose limestone formation, renowned in other places of the state for dinosaur tracks. Closer inspection of the cavern walls shows an intricate pattern of fossils that was laid down over sixty million years ago.

Mr. Ebell concludes the formal part of the tour at the edge of an underground river. Every assembly of water from a birdbath to an ocean inspires little boys. Likely as not, this inspiration translates as a barrage of rocks in honor of, and toward, the water. If you have a little boy that is easily inspired by water, let him know that Mr. Ebell does not appreciate this volley of veneration. Mr. Ebell is protective of his cave and scolds irreverence. He has conducted over thirty thousand trips through his cave, continues to make little discoveries, and is committed to preserving its beauty. Be sure and tell him what you think of his cave.

Unfortunately, a group of Boerne teenagers showed Mr. Ebell what they thought of his cave in early 1993. The repair costs for their attack on his cave were about $15,000. What took nature millions of years to create was damaged in minutes by vandals.

Mr. Ebell's address is 325 Kreutzberg Road, Boerne, Texas 78006. His phone number is (210) 537-4212.

ALONG THE WAY

In 1988 75 acres of Boerne City Park was set aside as **Cibolo Wilderness Trail**. It is on State Highway 46 (River Road), close to the rodeo arena, and alongside the baseball fields. There are picnic tables, drinking fountains, rest rooms, a little play area near one of the picnic tables, a pavilion, and the brand-spanking newly remodeled Cibolo Nature Center. A bulletin board on the front porch has notices about upcoming activities and volunteer opportunities.

All these accoutrements are there for the 4 miles of developed nature trails. The trails wind through a reclaimed marsh, a reestablished prairie, and a wooded creek bottom. My favorite is a tamped-down one-third mile along Cibolo Creek. Stately, knobby-kneed bald cypress trees crowd the banks. Huge slabs of limestone, wrenched at some remote time from the adjacent undercut bank, are strewn along the path. Towering cypress on one side and the limestone banks on the other make this trail feel like a secret.

Some parks have bird checklists for their visitors. Cibolo Wilderness Trail has a grass checklist or, as they put it, a Checklist of Potential Grasses. Lindheimer Muhly (*Muhlenbergia lindheimeri*) is on the list, as are about forty other types of grasses. Ferdinand Lindheimer (1801–79) was a German botanist who wandered through the area bounded by Austin, San Antonio, the San Saba River, and Enchanted Rock between 1836 and 1851 collecting and identifying plants. Twenty species of plants are named after him (*lindheimeri*).

Another German, Ferdinand von Roemer, traveled through much of the state and wrote a now-classic book about his "agreeable and rich memories." There are few people that I envy more than those who got to see Texas all fresh and sparkling. Roemer described Texas as a land of "wide, green prairies" and as a "beautiful land of meadows."

Only a few of these meadows remain, but at places like Cibolo Wilderness Trail, native grass meadows are being restored. Such a field of native grasses links us to an unspoiled time in our history—it gives us an anchor.

Other checklists are available for wildflowers, woody plants, and birds. These checklists are mailed to you if you become a Friend of the Cibolo Wilderness, along with a thrice-yearly newsletter telling about educational programs, guided hikes, and the family-oriented Fourth Saturday Programs. Cibolo Wilderness Trail is open every day from 8 A.M. to 10 P.M. The Nature Center is open on Saturday from 9 A.M. to 1 P.M. and on Sunday from 1 to 5 P.M. If you would like more information about the Fourth Saturday Programs or other events, call (210) 249-4616. There is no admission fee, but contributions to the Cibolo Wilderness Fund are not discouraged. The mailing address for Friends of the Cibolo Wilderness is P.O. Box 9, Boerne, Texas 78006.

Country Spirit Restaurant and Bar is at 707 South Main Street in Boerne in a house built in the 1870s. The menu has salads, soups, sandwiches, burgers, fajitas, and dinner entrées, including chicken-fried steak. For dieters, there is pasta, quiche, and marinated chicken. The dessert menu rounds up all the usual suspects like chocolate cake, apple pie, and cheesecake but throws in a ringer for the adults called margarita pie—oh, yes—and Blue Bell ice cream for the children. Country Spirit is open Sunday through Thursday from 11 A.M. to 9 P.M., on Friday and Saturday from 11 A.M. to 10 P.M., and, like Cave without a Name, is dark on Tuesdays. Call (210) 249-3607. $$$

Burnet
Cruising the Mighty Colorado

❂

You ask me what I like about Texas
I tell you it's the wide open spaces
Everything between the Sabine and the Rio Grande
It's the Llano Estacado, the Brazos, and the Colorado
It's the spirit of the people who share this land.
—Gary P. Nunn, "What I Like About Texas"

There are two Colorado Rivers. One cuts a deep, expansive ditch through Arizona. The other winds through vintage Texas Hill Country. The scenery from the deck of the Vanishing Texas River Cruise boat will bring tears to your eyes, but not because of cedar allergy. The tours operate year round. Excursions between the middle of November and the end of March have the bonus of bald eagle sightings.

The seventy-foot cruise boat's lower deck is enclosed and heated, but wear warm clothes during the winter. That way, you can strut around observation decks or sit on the foredeck feeling proud of our pretty state. Binoculars and reservations are, as they say, strongly recommended. So is this trip. Tours are daily except Tuesday at 11 A.M. and on weekends at 11 A.M. and 2:30 P.M. In September and December, tours are on Wednesdays and weekends only. Admission prices are about one-half the price of a ticket to a theme park. For reservations, call (512) 756-6986.

The **Vanishing Texas River Cruise** boat dock is in a cove on the northeastern shore of Lake Buchanan. It is reached by heading west on State Highway 29 from Burnet (population 3,504). After 3 miles, turn right (north) on State Road 2341. Drive 14 miles, turn left on a dirt road, pass over a cattle guard, and turn left onto an asphalt road, which descends to the dock.

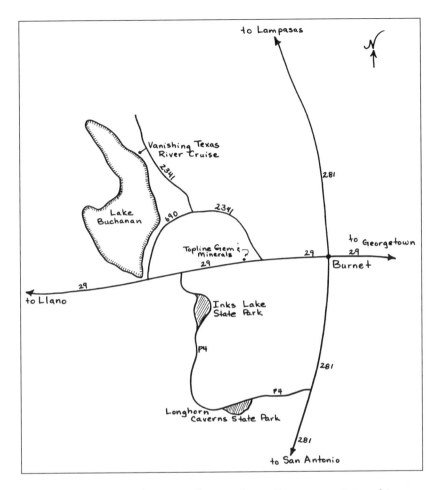

To assure a good seat on the tour boat, I suggest arriving thirty minutes before the departure time. The *Texas Eagle II*, the flagship of the Vanishing Texas River Cruise, is built to hold two hundred people and usually does. If you are going on a tour during the time of year to see the eagles (mid-November through March), take a seat on the lower deck, which is enclosed and heated. After the boat leaves the dock most people get up and mill around anyway. If you get cold, you will still have a warm place to light and sip hot coffee. That's having your lake and seating for it, too.

Lake level permitting, which it does except during a drought (when the river all but vanishes), the cruise crosses the northern part of Lake Buchanan and heads up the Colorado River. It passes limestone hills and bluffs, fifty-foot waterfalls, and juniper-clad Hill Country. The boat captain recites a brief history of the Lake Buchanan area and relates information about the Colorado River—for example, it starts in Lamesa and has a 48,000-square-mile watershed. I have no idea what that means. How do they know such things?

The captain also points out the birds: laughing gulls, ring-billed gulls, least terns, great blue herons, red-tailed hawks, and the double-crested cormorants with their orange throats and wispy, white crests. In recent years, even North American white pelicans, with their nine-foot wingspans, have been showing up on Lake Buchanan, although none of the range maps in bird books show swatches of color in Central Texas for North American pelicans. I guess birds don't read the books.

Wintering bald eagles (*Haliaeetus leucocephalus*) are the main drawing card for the Vanishing Texas River Cruise, and if you get to see only one it is worth the trip. Usually you see several eagles, both mature with white heads, white tails, and yellow beaks and immature, with dusky heads and tails, and dark beaks. You will spot them sitting in treetops and then lifting upward, with wingspans up to eight feet in the males and ten feet in females. Let me assure you that they have spotted you long before you spotted them; their vision is approximately fifteen times better than that of humans. Bald eagles can fly up to two hundred miles per hour. They live up to thirty-five years if they observe proper eating habits (by avoiding pesticides), get plenty of exercise (by having an unspoiled habitat in which to live and fly), and adopt a low-anxiety life-style (by steering clear of poachers).

Bald eagles are magnificent to watch. When they catch an updraft, they become free. After seeing a bald eagle in flight, its splayed-out and trussed-up appearance on the Great Seal of the United States is embarrassing. Someone needs to start a petition or draft a bill and get the seal changed. In fact, the Vanishing Texas River Cruise emblem would do nicely.

The cruise lasts about two and a half hours. There are rest rooms on board. Complimentary coffee and iced tea are available and, if you order it ahead of time, you can have a box lunch. I suggest bringing a light picnic lunch or a snack.

Talking about snacks reminds me of my family's first trip on the

Vanishing Texas River Cruise. My whole family met in Burnet to go on the cruise—Mom, Dad, my three younger sisters, and their husbands and children, my husband and I, and our children. We brought along a big thermos of hot coffee, loaves of homemade bread, and sliced cheddar cheese. As we passed by the little town of Tow (rhymes with "wow"), my brother-in-law turned to my sister, stretched out his arms, and declared, "A jug of coffee, a loaf of bread—and Tow." So goes a typical family gathering.

Other highlights of the 25-mile boat ride are artesian spring-fed Fall Creek Falls, which roughly marks the end of the lake and the beginning of the river, and the mushroomed limestone formations of Seldom Falls. Sheer red and gray limestone cliffs frame the river during some parts of the trip. The red deposits are tufa or sandstone, and the gray rock is Ellenburger limestone. These formations are around five hundred million years old and are part of the Llano uplift. And, then there is the lake itself. A little history review is in order.

The construction of **Buchanan Dam** started in 1929 but was interrupted by the Great Depression. The newly created Lower Colorado River Authority resumed construction in 1935, providing jobs for two thousand men in the depression-ravaged Hill Country. On May 20, 1937, the floodgates were closed and within two months the Colorado River dutifully sprawled to form Lake Buchanan. Ancient Indian hunting grounds and the remains of a hundred years of white settlement in the original Bluffton and Tow lay under the reddish water.

When one reads the history of these little settlements, the damming of a river takes on a human side. The book *Canyon of the Eagles: A History of Lake Buchanan and Official Guide to the Vanishing Texas River Cruise* by C. L. Yarbrough is available in the gift shop at the dock. It is worth the two hours or so it takes to read it. At times poignant and at other times horrifying, the history of the river is about ordinary people making extraordinary sacrifices and enduring extraordinary hardships. The following are excerpts from this compelling book:

> By 1936 the Great Depression had created in rural America an impoverished society in which there was no money and no realistic prospect of acquiring any. Almost all of the river people owned farms or small

ranches, but there was no market for their produce and no jobs to be had. For the first time in their lives, they were made to feel like poor people. When work at the dam started up again, virtually every man and boy in the valley showed up, hoping for a chance at non-stop, back-breaking sometimes dangerous labor that paid forty cents an hour if you were among the lucky ones. . . . Many of the men who stood day after day in these lines and slept there on the ground at night in order to be near the front of the line at daylight were men of property, reduced to doing anything they could to feed hollow-eyed children and put shoes on their feet come winter. . . . With cross-cut saws and axes, the timber cutters felled the ancient riverbottom forest of great pecan, live oak, burr oak and sycamore trees, many of which had stood for a thousand years. These men, who had taken great pride and joy in these ancient trees all of their lives, took no pleasure in their work; they were also clearing away their homes and their memories, all that they knew and loved.

Since I read the history of Lake Buchanan, man-made lakes look different to me—they look deeper somehow.

If Bluffton and Tow look to a rich past, nearby Burnet looks to a rich future. Its growth curve promises to steepen with a weekend steam train line from Austin, a fledgling Hamilton Creek walkway and park, a new forty-two–bed hospital, an extended airport runway, a growing number of community college courses, and an eighteen-hole municipal golf course. Add to these its hunting and recreational opportunities and its proximity to Austin, and Burnet may stand accused of overindulging in Wheaties.

For now, though, Burnet is a little town with a little town square and little town stores and little town friendliness. My favorite place to buy clothes is on the square in Burnet. Tell owner Sue Mallett of **Suzie Q** that one of the Denney girls sent you. She will give you special attention. But, then, she would have anyway. Call her at (512) 756-8246.

AREA INTERESTS

Mallards are near the boat dock of the Vanishing Texas River Cruise. They are so intense when you feed them old bread.

Fall Creek, Lake Buchanan

Riverwalk Cafe is on Highway 29 West in Burnet. This family restaurant is owned and operated by Alan and Sherrye McAnelly, a Houston couple that said, "Let's git," and left the big city. They are immensely happy with their decision to rear their children in Burnet and, in return, serve excellent food to all-comers. The large menu offers appetizers like fried cheese and fried mushrooms with gravy, burgers and sandwiches, chicken, catfish, chicken-fried steak, chopped sirloin, rib eye steaks, and pork chops. Sherrye bakes pies every day. Get her to show you her blue ribbons. For the dieter, there are salads, a vegetable plate, and marinated, grilled chicken breast on rice pilaf. The Riverwalk Cafe opens every day at 7 A.M. to serve breakfast and closes at 9 P.M. on weekdays and at 10 P.M. on Friday and Saturday. Call (512) 756-4100. $$

Topline Gem and Minerals is located on Highway 29 West, 2 miles past the turnoff to the Vanishing Texas River Cruise, or 5 miles past the intersection of Highways 29 and 281. Owner Dolphe Planche will let you pick out a geode for a few dollars and cut it in half for another dollar. Call (512) 756-6253. Open during the day unless Mr. Planche is at a rock and mineral show.

The **Hill Country Flyer,** a passenger steam train, leaves Cedar Park, just north of Austin, at 10 A.M. on Saturdays and Sundays and arrives in Burnet at noon for a three-hour layover. I have done both, and it is more fun to see it arrive and depart than to be on board. That is a personal bias that is generated by my frustration at being unable to stop and look at stuff when I am on a train or, for that matter, a bus or a plane. A friend of mine, Gardner Sumner, thoroughly enjoyed his ride on the steam train, but then he manages to make an adventure out of almost anything he does. For reservation information call (512) 477-8468. The train ride is a bit pricey and hot in the summer, unless you are in one of the more expensive air-conditioned cars. (But, wouldn't an air-conditioned car miss the whole point of riding a steam train?)

Inks Lake State Park on Park Road 4 between Burnet and Marble Falls could fill a chapter by itself. It is a popular, twelve hundred–acre park on the eastern shore of Inks Lake, another wide spot in the Colorado River. Trailer, tent, and walk-in campsites, screened shelters, group facilities, picnic tables, playgrounds, boat ramps, swimming areas, fishing piers, hiking trails, paddle boat and canoe rentals, a nine-hole golf course, and ducks to feed cover all the bases. There is even a grocery store that, with just about everything else, has dollar-sacks of animal feed for the ducks and deer.

Inks Lake State Park has swimming areas for the three classes of lake swimmers: (1) waders, (2) bottom-touchers, and (3) treaders who hate to touch the slimy, gooey mud because it oozes between your toes and might contain snakes and other imagined absurdities. I am among the latter and, therefore, prefer Devil's Waterhole at the northeast end of the camping area. Children need to wear life jackets, because it is quite deep and there are no lifeguards. But there are nice gneiss overhangs, sycamore trees, and limestone beaches that go to the water's edge. Spring Creek feeds into Devil's Waterhole and is a geologically stimulating area for a short hike.

A second swimming area is across the inlet from the grocery store and satisfies the wading and bottom-touching crowd. Picnic tables, a playground, rest rooms, and a grassy area without fire ants are nearby.

From Burnet, take Highway 29 West toward Llano. After 9 miles, turn left (south) on Park Road 4 and go 3 miles to the park entrance.

Hill Country Flyer

From Marble Falls, take Highway 281 North toward Burnet. After 8 miles, turn left (west) on Park Road 4 and go 12 miles to the park entrance.

For reservations call (512) 389-8900 (see Appendix 1). For other information contact Park Superintendent, Inks Lake State Park, Route 2, Box 31, Burnet, Texas 78611, or call (512) 793-2223, 8 A.M. to 5 P.M., daily. State park admission fees apply.

Longhorn Cavern State Park is also on Park Road 4, 6 miles off of Highway 281 and 9 miles off of Highway 29. This 629-acre park is for day use only and is open from dawn to dusk every day except Christmas Eve and Christmas Day. Tours through Longhorn Cavern (64° year round) are conducted every day at the following times: during spring (March, April, and May), Monday through Friday, every hour from 10 A.M. to 4 P.M., on Saturday and Sunday, every hour from 10 A.M. to 5 P.M.; during summer (Memorial Day through Labor Day), every hour from 10 A.M. to 6 P.M.; during winter (the rest of the year), Monday through Friday at 10:30 A.M., 1 P.M., and 3 P.M., on Saturday and Sunday, every hour from 10 A.M. to 5 P.M. If I were you, I would call ahead at (512) 756-6976. The tours last about one hour and twenty-five minutes.

Our tour through Longhorn Cavern was a memorable experience, but not for the usual reasons. The cavern itself is interesting, if you like to stoop and squeeze through the interconnecting passageways of a human-sized ant farm. The cavern was formed by water which slowly scooped and dissolved a labyrinth in five hundred million-year-old Ellenburger limestone. There are also a few dripstone and rimstone deposits, massive deposits of calcite crystals, and ample evidence of the thousand-year history of human use. The cavern extends for some 15 miles, but the tour is limited to 1.25 miles. Thank goodness.

Our tour group consisted of three patient, chatty grandmas with their eleven grandchildren, a bellowing woman who said, "Well, I'll be dawged" approximately fifty times, a man who had not recently bathed, and the others of us who stampeded for the tunnel exit at the end of the tour. (Perhaps another tour on another day would have prompted me to heartily recommend this cavern as a fresh and quiet respite from the city's noise and smog.) Ticket prices are very reasonable and holders of a Texas Conservation Passport receive a discount.

Frankly, we much preferred the park's half-mile self-guided nature trail and one-and-a-half-mile hiking trail. Trail guidebooks are available at the visitor's center. The trails go through stands of oak and juniper trees, over surface exposures of gray, Ellenburger limestone, and past bushes of lantana.

Comfort
Visiting a Bat Roost

❂

And it stretches on forever
Through a thousand little towns
With their stores all dark and silent
And their flashing yellow lights,
And nobody sees you passing
In the fury of your flight.
—James McMurtry, "Crazy Wind"

Comfort (population 1,548) is noted for antique shops; however, an abandoned railroad tunnel near Comfort (**Old Tunnel Wildlife Management Area**) is the hand-picked haunt of several million warm-blooded relics. In his book *America's Neighborhood Bats,* Dr. Merlin Tuttle claims that "bat fossils have been found that date back approximately 50 million years, but surprisingly, the bats of that ancient period very closely resembled those we know today."

With that information and blurring of the distinction between antique relics and fossil relics, you can truthfully boast, "We went antiquing in Comfort." Thus avoided is an awkward silence at the next meeting of the Junior League or Kiwanis Club when you otherwise would have said, "We visited a bat roost."

The directions to the bat roost seem complicated when you read them, but are actually easy to follow. The bats are not going to wait on you to start the show, so allow plenty of travel time—about two hours from the Alamo and two hours and forty-five minutes from the Capitol.

To reach the bat roost, exit Interstate Highway 10 at State Highway 87 North and turn left (south) toward Comfort. Coming from

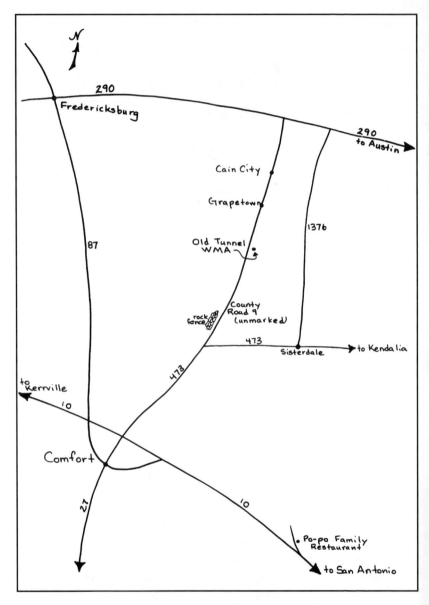

San Antonio, this is the second Comfort exit. A mile past the Dairy Queen, turn left (east) on Farm Road 473, which is the road to Sisterdale. This road will pass back under IH-10. On the right you will see a white wooden structure that looks like a Dutch windmill without blades. This is the Steves' bat roost, and it is on private property.

Continue 5 miles in a northeasterly direction on FM 473 until you reach a **Y** in the road. To the right (due east) is the road to Sisterdale. Do not turn here, but continue north on unmarked County Road 9 for another 8 miles.

At the top of a long, curving hill is a sign "Alamo Springs Subdivision" and a stand of mailboxes. (If you continue north on this road for about 9 miles, you will eventually reach U.S. Highway 290 through Cain City, but it is a tricky negotiation, especially in the dark. It is a worthwhile Sunday spin in good light, though.)

Anyway, back at the mailboxes, there is parking space and a plaque letting you know that you are where you thought you were. Be quiet. The bats are napping inside the tunnel.

Central Texas' only railroad tunnel was completed in 1913 and was the midpoint of the Fredericksburg and Northern's 23-mile line between Comfort and Fredericksburg. The line operated until the Great Depression and was dismantled in 1942. Since then, Mexican free-tailed bats (*Tadarida brasiliensis*) and smaller numbers of cave bats (*Myotis velifer*) have roosted in the tunnel from March to October.

Bats are born in June, one to a litter, and placed in safe places—usually ceilings of caves or cave-like areas—in wiggling, pink clusters. The babies grow fur, learn to fly, and, by the middle of the summer, join their mothers for the evening hunt. Recent studies by Mirian Bailey, a graduate student of Dr. John Baccus, director of wildlife biology at Southwest Texas State University, indicate that the railroad tunnel near Comfort is not a nursery colony (mothers and their newborns). Instead, it is a mixed population of non-lactating females, lactating females, males, and, later in the summer, juvenile bats. This is in contrast to some of the other bat caves in the region (Bracken Cave and Kickapoo Cavern) that are nursery colonies. The population mixture at the railroad tunnel was a surprising find since it had always been assumed that the railroad tunnel was a nursery colony.

Every evening the bats leave the railroad tunnel to eat moths and flying ants and beetles and bugs. It is estimated that Mexican free-tailed bats eat one-quarter to one-half of their weight in insects every day. Given that roughly one hundred million bats of this species alone

Rock fence near Old Tunnel Wildlife Management Area

spend the summer in Texas, most of them in the Edwards Plateau, it is surprising that moths still exist. (Perhaps, they recoup their losses when the bats go to Mexico for the winter.)

Showtime is dusk. Admission is free. There are two galleries: the first is a wooden deck adjacent to the parking area; the second is at the end of an easily followed trail that starts at the parking area and leads to what could be called the west mezzanine level. From this vantage point, you can actually peer down into the tunnel from a ridge above the tunnel entrance. The second area is open to visitors only two evenings per week (Thursday and Saturday) because of possible visitor impact on the bats' exit patterns. A Texas Parks and Wildlife Department guide is at the tunnel every evening.

The show's warm-up act is hungry hawks, circling above the tunnel entrance. One bat emerges, then another, then small groups. Soon they whirl out by the thousands in a thick, pungent, squeaky cloud. The hawks catch a few. This crepuscular flight from the end of the tunnel is moderately spectacular. (My journalist mother has told me a million times not to exaggerate.) Had I not read Dr. Tuttle's book, I would have been concerned about catching rabies or having a vicious bat muss my hair.

Not to worry. Dr. Tuttle points out: "Less than a half of 1 percent of bats contract rabies, a frequency no higher than that seen in many other mammals. Like others, they die quickly, but unlike even dogs and cats, rabid bats seldom become aggressive. . . . rabid bats seldom transmit rabies to any animals except other bats." Still, Mexican free-tailed bats are susceptible to rabies, and ones on the ground might be sick; caution children about this situation.

ALONG THE WAY

Po-Po Family Restaurant was originally built as a dance hall. Although the mailing address is in Boerne, this "Texas tradition since 1929" is reached by taking the Welfare Exit from Interstate Highway 10 West. It is on the right, less than a mile from the exit. Steaks, chicken-fried steak, fried catfish, and fried chicken are the main draws. The menu also offers leaner choices of grilled chicken and home-style vegetables. Po-Po's is open seven days a week from 11 A.M. to 9:30 P.M. It is wise (no, let's say necessary) to make reservations on the weekends. Call (210) 537-4194 and (210) 537-4399. $$

Unless you plan to drive like a bat, as the saying goes, allow forty-five minutes driving time from Po-Po's to the railroad tunnel. You will be unable to—in alphabetical order—clip, rip, whip, or zip over the last few miles to the tunnel, because of the jolting possibility of running across a deer or another car on the narrow road.

Along County Road 9, there is a half-mile stretch of **rock fence.** Built a century or more ago, rock fences such as these can be found throughout the Texas Hill Country. This fence is particularly solid evidence of German industry in the mid-1800s. Roy Bedichek, the late Texas naturalist, talks about stone fences in these words:

Sections of the noble fences, especially those available to highways, should be preserved, not only because they are beautiful in and of themselves, but because their testimony is significant of a period which will grow in historical importance, century by century, as long as present civilization endures. The blocks composing these structures are crumblings off the great limestone ledges, vertebrae of the hillsides, quarried by the swelling roots of a vegetation starved for any pitiful little pocket of moisture or bit of nourishment stingily stored in natural creases and seams of rock.

Fredericksburg
Picking Peaches for a Cobbler

And you better run take hold
You're gonna' get young 'fore they get old
And them Texas women is Texas gold
With kisses that are sweeter than cactus.
—Willis Alan Ramsey, "Northeast Texas Women"

Anne (pronounced "Annie") Mae Glimp makes a peach cobbler that is worth cutting in line for. If you're one of the first in line, you get to eat some of Mrs. Glimp's cobbler. If you're not one of the first in line, you wish you had been. Once you have tasted her cobbler, you will understand why she wins blue ribbons in county baking contests.

Mrs. Glimp lives in a white frame house about ten miles east of Burnet. Her sheep farm and peach orchard are about a mile down the road from my parents' ranch. Mrs. Glimp is my hero. When I am in a tight spot, and I don't know which way to turn, I ask myself, "What would Mrs. Glimp do?" The rock generally moves.

To make Mrs. Glimp's cobbler, you need fresh peaches. Canned won't do. Frozen won't do either, unless you put them up yourself last summer. In season, roadside stands and some grocery stores sell good peaches; however, if you want a blue ribbon cobbler, you must pick your own fruit. Two orchards in Fredericksburg do fine.

Fredericksburg (population 7,256) has an unmistakable German slant and is a popular destination for those who like bakeries, fine restaurants, museums, historic buildings, unusual shops, art galleries, and a wide Main Street. Of the hundred or so towns in Texas with a German name, German ethos is nowhere more apparent than in Fredericksburg.

However, don't go to Fredericksburg expecting to see lederhosen-

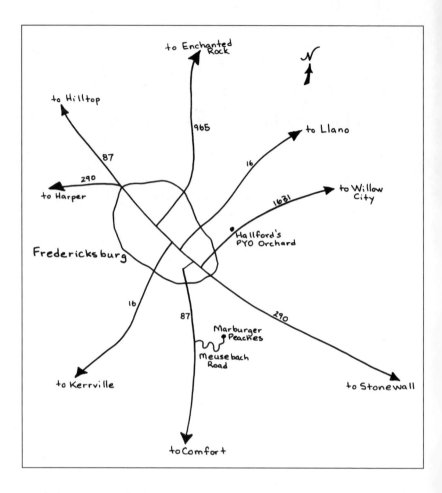

clad men, arms locked and swaying, singing *Du, Du Liegst Mir Im Herzen*. Fredericksburg respects its German heritage; it doesn't strain toward it. A glance at German history in Texas might explain this distinction.

Among the cultural traits of German people is respect approaching reverence for the land. It was desire for land that brought the first wave of German immigrants to Texas in the 1830s and 1840s. Europe had too little land for too many people, and tales of a beautiful and wide-open place called Texas tickled the wanderlust. Many of the immigrants were small farmers squeezed out of their homeland's pastoral picture by the development of large-scale commercial agriculture. Others were artisans and small-business owners who simply could not compete with the emerging giants of modern industry.

Although a faraway place called Texas offered the opportunity to recreate a premodern Germany, courage and determination were required to deal with Texas floods and droughts, the isolation of the frontier, and the Comanches. But the German immigrants planted their feet and their crops and they stayed. When they learned that their land grant occupied nonnegotiable Comanche hunting grounds, they took the obvious course—they negotiated anyway.

Remembered also for his contribution to German colonization efforts in Texas, John O. Meusebach is best known for negotiating a peace treaty with chiefs Buffalo Hump, Santana, and Old Owl. Signed in 1847 and called the Meusebach-Comanche Treaty, this agreement opened up 3,878,000 acres for settlement. It was honored by both parties—the Meusebach-Comanche Treaty was the only major Indian treaty that was never broken.

The German-Texans may have peacefully coexisted with their Comanche neighbors, but they did not always fare as well with their Anglo-American neighbors. For reasons that were hard for other Texans to understand, some German-Texans opposed slavery and secession. Anti-German hostility resulted. The world wars again tested the ties that bound other Texans to their neighbors of German ancestry. German-Texans proved where their loyalties lay. Among those who served in the American armed forces during World War II was Fredericksburg-born Fleet Admiral Chester Nimitz, commander-in-chief of the Pacific. A museum honoring the two million men and women who served under Nimitz is in the **Admiral Nimitz Museum and Historical Center** at 328 East Main in Fredericksburg. It is the building that looks like a steamboat.

But, I was going to talk about peaches.

There are many peach varieties. Some ripen as early as mid-May, others as late as mid-September. Those ripening early, like Springold and Bicentennial, are called cling peaches. The edible part of the peach clings like the very devil to the pit. Peaches that ripen in June and July, the freestone varieties, are somewhat easier to work with since the fruit is easily freed from the pit or stone.

Varieties with names like Red Globe, Majestic, and Dixiland are

Bauer's Antique Toy Museum, Fredericksburg

the favorites of seasoned peach pickers. On "freestone weekends" pick-your-own (PYO) orchards can become crowded. You might chance it, but a phone call ahead would be wise. Both of the orchards discussed in this section accept reservations.

In early spring the *Fredericksburg Standard Radio Post* publishes a free visitors' guide, which includes, along with other information about Fredericksburg, a list of self-serve orchards in the area. This guide is available at the newspaper office at 108 East Main Street and at many of the area businesses while, as they say, supplies last. Of the dozen or so PYO orchards in the Fredericksburg area, I have found two that I think are best-fruited for families: Hallford's Pick Your Own Orchard and Marburger Orchard.

Hallford's Pick Your Own Orchard is 1 mile from East Main Street on FM Road 1631 (Cave Creek Road). The telephone number is (210) 997-3064. The Hallford Orchard is owned and operated by the E. W. Hallford family. About one hundred acres of peach trees are there for the picking from late May through July or until the fruit is gone. The orchard is open 8 A.M. to 6 P.M. Monday through Saturday, noon to 6 P.M. on Sunday.

When you arrive at the orchard shed, you are offered slices of the varieties of ripe peaches that are available for picking that day. You are given nice, clean, half-bushel cardboard boxes with "PEACHES" written on the side and directions to the peach-heavy trees. Drive to the rows of trees that you plan to pick. Harvesting done, return to the shed and pay the keeper of the peach boxes. Prices vary with supply and demand, but are around $10 to $15 per half-bushel.

Peaches are the primary appeal, but depending on the season, you can also pick your own nectarines and blackberries or cut your own Christmas tree. A hint: trees are sold during December, but people who want the perfect tree tag their selection much earlier. This strategy might be confusing to a small child when, in the middle of July, you announce that it is time to pick out a Christmas tree.

Marburger Orchard is 5 miles south of Fredericksburg on U.S. Highway 87, heading toward Comfort. Turn east on Meusebach (the Texas pronunciation rhymes with "noisy track") Road and follow the signs, making right angle and hairpin turns, for about 1.5 miles to the orchard shed.

Like Hallford's, you are offered a sample of the ripe peaches. You leave your car at the shed and walk a short distance to the pickable trees. When you are through, someone will roar away in a trailer contraption and bring your peaches to the shed. Hours of operation are the same as Hallford, 8 A.M. to 6 P.M., Monday through Saturday, noon to 6 P.M. on Sunday. The phone number is (210) 997-9433.

AREA INTERESTS

Vereins Kirche is to Fredericksburg what the Capitol is to Austin and the Alamo is to San Antonio. Within the eight-sided, coffee mill–shaped confines of this museum is a compact, systematic history lesson about Fredericksburg and Gillespie County. Connections with Deutschland are still apparent—a broken piece of the Berlin Wall is proudly displayed on a table in the middle of the museum.

Two Germans were visiting the Vereins Kirche the day I was there. Hans Bergner, a native of Fredericksburg, was the keeper of the coffee mill that day. To the delight of his German visitors and the one from San Antonio who was eavesdropping, Herr Bergner conducted the museum tour *auf Deutsch*. Vereins Kirche is located on Market

Vereins Kirche, Fredericksburg

Square on West Main Street near the middle of town. It is open from
10 A.M. to 2 P.M., Monday through Friday, October through February. A nominal fee is charged. The phone number is (210) 997-7832.
The Main Book Shop is at its new location next to the
Fredericksburg Bakery at 143 East Main Street. This is a first-rate
bookstore with a large selection of children's books, cookbooks, and
books about Texas. It is open Monday through Friday, 9 A.M. to
5:30 P.M., on Saturday from 9:30 A.M. to 5:30 P.M., and Sunday from
1 P.M. to 5 P.M. The book shop's phone numbers are (210) 997-2375
and (800) 225-2375.

Bauer's Antique Toy Museum has over two thousand toys which
fill a high-ceilinged room and span a century of American toys. From
Cracker Jack prizes to an 1885 Victor bicycle, everyone can spot an
old favorite amid Don Bauer's life's treasures. It is located at 223 East
Main Street and is open every day from 10 A.M. to 5 P.M. (or, as Mr.
Bauer says, "except when the street is empty.") Mr. Bauer welcomes
groups and will gladly open his museum during the evening or "when-
ever," with just a phone call ahead of time. There is no admission
fee, but donations are accepted. You can call Mr. Bauer at (210) 997-
9394.

Of **collectibles and collectables,** spelled either way, Fredericksburg
probably has it in one of its shops. You can find everything from an
Apache war bonnet to a zebra rug, dulcimers, Amish quilts, patterns
for German dirndls, tea-dyed dolls, and musical glow balls. There is
even an item called, and I quote, a mounted chicken in a basket.
Right there on Main Street, a mounted chicken in a basket.

Ken Hall and Company Texas Barbecue is just south of
Fredericksburg on U.S. Highway 87. Fredericksburg is full of
wunderbar restaurants and charming cafes. Thanks anyway, but I'll
be ordering a chopped beef sandwich at the counter and pulling a
longneck from a tub of ice at Ken Hall's place. The owner is one of
those legends in his own time. He is considered the best high school
football player ever. He holds numerous schoolboy football records
set between 1950 and 1953. And he is just as nice and friendly as he
can be. Above framed newspaper clippings of his high school glory
days is this quote: "No one can go back and make a brand new start,
my friend, but anyone can start from here and make a brand new

end." Mr. Hall's restaurant is open from 11 A.M. to 8:30 P.M. every day except Monday. The phone number is (210) 997-2353. Good stuff. $$

Other area interests are Enchanted Rock and Stonewall, which have their own sections.

MRS. GLIMP'S PEACH COBBLER

Line the sides and bottom of a 9 x 12 pan with one-inch strips of pie dough. Prepare cobbler by combining 2 quarts of sliced peaches, fresh or frozen (thawed, of course) with 2 cups of sugar, 1 stick of butter, 2 tablespoons of flour, and the juice of 1/2 lemon. Cook on medium heat until it is "the right consistency for cobbler." Cool for a little while and pour into prepared crust. Cover the top with one-inch strips of pie dough, and sprinkle top with cinnamon sugar. Cook at 350° for 50 to 60 minutes or until "crust is done on top." Important note: My brother-in-law suggests topping warm cobbler with a scoop or two of Blue Bell vanilla ice cream. (Yessiree, bobwhite.)

Goliad
Flowers and Soldiers

This is the only place on earth bluebonnets grow
Once a year they come and go
At this old house here by the road
And, when we die we say we'll catch some blackbird's wing
And, we will fly away together
Come some sweet bluebonnet spring.
—Nanci Griffith, "Gulf Coast Highway"

Ask any Texan and, for that matter, most Americans about the Battle of the Alamo and they will solemnly tell the story. They will mention Travis and Bowie and Bonham and Crockett. They will tell of Santa Anna's demand for surrender and William B. Travis's cannon shot answer. They will tell of Travis drawing a line in the dirt and all but one man stepping across. And they will tell of a battle with thirty-to-one odds that ended in death for every Alamo defender. All 189 of them. The Alamo is the cornerstone of a proud Texas heritage and we know the story.

But ask a Texan about Goliad and the answer might be: "That's the one where they drew the black beans, I think." The massacre that occurred near Goliad during the Texas Revolution was not the one where they drew the black beans. The incident involving black beans happened six years later under a very different set of circumstances. Almost twice as many Texas volunteers were slaughtered at Goliad than died defending the Alamo. Why don't we remember the details? Because, a series of tragic misjudgments lie behind the Goliad massacre, and God love us, Texans choose to overlook the flaws in our history.

Before you visit Presidio La Bahía, you should know the story. The first part of this chapter is a retelling of the history of the Goliad massacre.

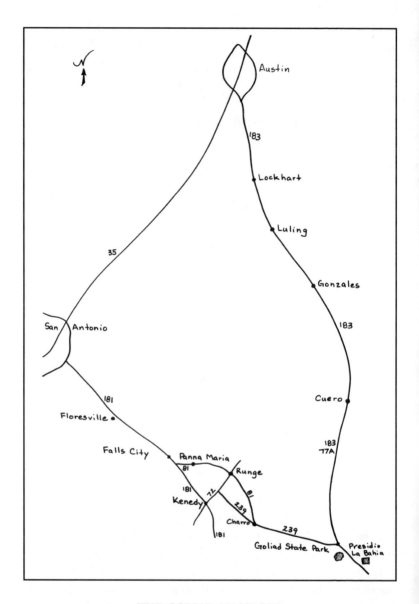

THE GOLIAD MASSACRE

About four hundred volunteers, only about a dozen of whom were Texas settlers, were under the command of Col. James Walker Fannin at Presidio La Bahía, the fortress at Goliad. Bitter that the volunteers had not been "sustained in a proper manner," Fannin was prompted by the advance of the Mexican force to write a letter to Texas' Acting

Governor James Robinson on March 1, 1836, asking permission to abandon La Bahía. Robinson's reply was characteristic of the disorganized and indecisive General Council in San Felipe: Fannin could stay or go, whatever he thought best. Bowing to his rowdy volunteer army's whim, Fannin delayed his men's departure from La Bahía until March 19.

Although Fannin knew that Col. José Urrea's army was in pursuit, he chose to lug heavy artillery, slowing his retreat. Urrea caught up with the Texas force within a half-mile of a small woods that would have given them some cover. An ammunition cart broke down, but instead of leaving it and rushing for the woods, Fannin allowed his men to stop and try to fix it. The Mexican army wasted no time in surrounding them.

The Texans hurriedly formed a square, and what came to be known in the history books as the Battle of Coleto Creek began. The fighting continued until sunset. By nightfall seven volunteers were dead and sixty were wounded. Among the wounded was their commander, Colonel Fannin. Exhausted and surrounded by the enemy, the Texas volunteers discovered that no one had remembered to bring along any water.

By the following morning, the Mexican army had received reinforcements and outnumbered the Texans nearly seven to one. About two hundred Texans were able-bodied, but exhausted and thirsty. Fannin had the unenviable choice of making a stand, rushing for the woods and leaving the wounded behind, or surrendering. After talking it over with his officers, he chose to surrender if "honorable capitulation would be granted." Fannin took along an interpreter and signed a treaty with Urrea. The terms of the surrender, as understood by the Texans and ultimately by the people of the United States, were those of honorable capitulation; however, the surrender was unconditional. General Urrea may have told Fannin that his men would be treated humanely, and Fannin certainly let his men think that such was the case, but the Texans were "surrendered at discretion."

The men stacked their arms and were marched back to La Bahía. Santa Anna denied Urrea's request for leniency for the Texas prisoners. On Palm Sunday, March 27, 1836, the prisoners who were able to walk were divided into three groups, marched in different directions from the fort, and shot by firing squad. The Mexican soldiers then returned to the fort and bayoneted and shot the wounded. Colonel Fannin was the last to die.

Their bodies were piled and burned. Two months later, their remains were gathered and buried in a common grave. A granite memorial was erected at the site in 1939.

Presidio La Bahía is an imposing reminder of the brave volunteers who died in defense of liberty. Indeed, unlike the Alamo defenders, the Texas volunteers at Goliad knew that independence from Mexico had been declared. Presidio La Bahía is on the southwest bank of the San Antonio River. About three and one-half acres are surrounded by stone walls which are three feet thick and between eight and ten feet tall. Its massive walls have been restored to the 1836 appearance through generous grants from the Kathryn O'Connor Foundation. It is an authentic restoration and is the best example in Texas of a Spanish fort. The Presidio and its museum are operated by the Diocese of Victoria Catholic Church.

The nearby granite memorial may be the official grave site of Fannin and his men, but Presidio La Bahía is a better place to pay homage. Visit Our Lady of Loreto Chapel, where they were sequestered for a week as they awaited an unknown fate. Climb the parapets and gaze over the fields where they were cut down by firing squad. In the spring, the time of year that they were massacred, the fields are covered with wildflowers. These flowers answer the question of the 1960s antiwar anthem: "Where have all the flowers gone?" And, by answering that old question, they implore us to remember the men who died at Goliad.

John Collins found the words for all of us at the June 4, 1986, sesquicentennial address at the Fannin Memorial: "Brave men die more than just once. In our minds we have buried these men again and again. Some of us here are descendants of the men that lie beneath this monument, but they are ancestors to all of us. We share a common destiny today as Texans because we are inheritors of their sacrifice. They gave their lives for a future they would never see, for a people they would never know—you and me."

Presidio La Bahía is located 1 mile south of Goliad on U.S. Highway 183. It is open from 9 A.M. to 4:45 P.M. daily. Admission price is

Mission Espíritu Santo de Zuñiga, Goliad

a few dollars. There is a gift shop. For more information, write P.O. Box 57, Goliad, Texas 77963, or call (512) 645-3752.

IN THE AREA AND ALONG THE WAY

On the way to Presidio La Bahía on U.S. Highway 183, you will pass by the entrance to **Goliad State Park,** the site of the reconstructed **Mission Espíritu Santo de Zuñiga** (Mission of Our Lady of the Holy Spirit of Zuñiga). Espíritu Santo was a Spanish colonial mission established in the mid-1700s by the Franciscan order to Spaniardize the local Indians.

By 1931, when the Texas Legislature created Goliad State Park, senescence, a couple of tornadoes (including one in 1902 that killed 114 people), and recycling of building stones by local residents had reduced the mission, its outbuildings, and the perimeter wall to a little pile of rocks. Yet, under supervision of the National Park Service, the Goliad city council rebuilt the main structures for use as a public school. The buildings were later

Prickly pear, Goliad Nature Trail

used by Aranama College to educate Spanish-speaking Texans.

Today you will see the reconstructed Mission Espíritu Santo on a dignified little hill overlooking the entrance to Goliad State Park. What was once the granary serves as a museum. Interpretive exhibits detail the Spanish quest to Christianize the Karankawa, Cujane, and Coapite Indians. The Franciscan monks enjoyed only nominal success in curing souls, but their cattle herds were fruitful and multiplied—the mission's herds numbered nearly 40,000 during the mid-1800s. The Indians and civilians eventually strayed from the fold, taking the cattle with them. In 1862 the mission closed.

Goliad State Park has a one-third–mile self-guided nature trail that starts near the mission. Plans exist to extend the trail to the historic district of downtown Goliad (population 2,026). At this writing, the trail is confined to the woodlands of the San Antonio River bottom-land with sycamore, cottonwood, and pecan trees, and a chaparral, or thornbrush country, with prickly pear cactus, mesquite, and huisache.

Honey mesquite trees are often ignored because they are so common and maligned as a prominent actor in the brush invasion of the South Texas plains. Brush invasion resulted from overgrazing, grassfire prevention, and seed dispersal by livestock. Despised by stockmen because it competes with range grass, mesquite (*Prosopis glandulosa*) deserves a few kind remarks. Golden-fronted woodpeckers (*Centurus aurifrons*) nest in holes in mesquite trees and return to the same tree year after year. Mesquite trees provide shade and concealment for deer, javelina, and quail. Deer, quail, and jackrabbits also feed on its seeds and leaves. Finally, because its roots contain nitrogen-fixing bacteria, mesquite trees enrich the soil.

Prickly pear (*Opuntia*) cacti are also taken for granted. Not only are the flowers beautiful and varied and the fruits suitable for making jelly, but these cacti provide cover for small animals, and their flat branches (pads) are edible all year long. During severe droughts, like the one during the late 1940s and early 1950s, ranchers burned off the spines and glochids for forage for their cattle. In his novel *The Time It Never Rained*, Elmer Kelton described how this was done:

> Since the time when Texas was still a part of Mexico, Mexican cart men had fed prickly pear to their oxen on the long trails during the wintertime. They would break off the thorny pads and hold them over a flame on a stick or a pitchfork to burn off the sharp spines. In later years Anglo stockmen had devised more efficient types of prickly pear burners, starting first with kerosene, developing gradu-ally to butane units fueled from a tank on a pickup bed or truck. Resembling a military flamethrower, the device spewed a long, white-hot tongue of flame which in seconds curled the thorns and left only spots of white ash. Sheep and cattle learned to follow the men, eating the hot green pear leaves as a belly-filler in place of grass and hay.

Mission Espíritu Santo de Zuñiga and the nature trail with the now better-appreciated mesquite and prickly pear are on the grounds of Goliad State Park. The mission is open from 8 A.M. to 12 noon and from 1 P.M. to 5 P.M. daily. Admission to the park requires the usual state park fee or is free for holders of the Texas Conservation Passport (see Appendix 1). For more information, write P.O. Box 727, Goliad, Texas 77963, or call (512) 645-3405.

Floresville (population 5,349) has a giant peanut on the Wilson County Courthouse square. To take a picture of the kids standing beside it and grinning, exit Business 181 about 5 miles north of Floresville.

Shorty's Cafe in **Falls City** (population 493) is the place to be if it's lunchtime (dinnertime in the local vernacular), or if it's time for a generous slice of fresh homemade pie. The menu includes grilled chicken breast and green beans, chicken-fried steak, and other staples, even chicken gizzards. The cafe is on Highway 181 South at Falls City and is open from 10:30 A.M. to 10:30 P.M. Call them at (210) 254-3322. $$

And, if you need food for the spirit, take a side trip to the **Immaculate Conception Catholic Church** in **Panna Maria** (population 96), the oldest Polish settlement in the United States. The chalice and hand-carved chairs used during the 1987 papal mass in San Antonio are exhibited in this little church because that is what the Pope said he wanted done with it. (The present Pope is Polish and he picked the people of Panna Maria to protect and keep these items.) The first Immaculate Conception Church at Panna Maria was built at this site in 1856. Lightning destroyed it, and the new church was built during 1877 and 1878. This one has, so far, been spared the thunderbolt and the swarm of locusts.

U.S. Highway 181 to Goliad is a top pick for a **spring wildflower drive.** We have the State Department of Highways and Public Transportation to thank for our highway wildflowers. Over one million acres of right-of-way are part of what the late Texas naturalist Roy Bedichek called the "far-reaching arboretums." In the 1930s Texas became the first state to develop a plan to use native plants along the road. Since the mid-1980s, 1 percent of the construction costs of a new highway is earmarked for landscaping. For the free brochure *Wildflowers of Texas,* write Travel and Information Division, State Department of Highways and Public Transportation, P.O. Box 5064, Austin, Texas 78763-5064.

Johnson City
Purdy Places on the Pedernales

❂

See how it sparkles in my eyes
I couldn't hide it if I tried—that's right
I don't love you much do I
Just more than anything else in this whole world.
—Guy Clark and Richard Leigh, "I Don't Love You Much Do I"

Texas place names would be less troublesome if all were as straight-forward as Llano, San Saba, and Lampasas. Llano County's county seat is Llano and the through-running river is the Llano River. San Saba is the county seat of San Saba and is beside the San Saba River. And Lampasas County's center of government is Lampasas, right there beside the Lampasas River.

By contrast, let us consider Johnson. Johnson City (population 959) is the county seat of Blanco County and is at a bend in the Pedernales River. Johnson County is nearly 200 miles away from Johnson City. Lake Lyndon B. Johnson is in Llano County, the Lyndon B. Johnson State and National Parks are in Gillespie County, the Lyndon B. Johnson Space Center is near Houston, and the Lyndon B. Johnson Library is in Austin.

In keeping with that trend, except in passing (through), this chapter has little to do with Johnson City. This chapter is about three places on the Pedernales River: Hamilton Pool, Westcave Preserve, and Pedernales Falls State Park. Johnson City just happens to be the last town of any size on the Pedernales River before it unthreads into the Colorado River.

"Purdy" in the title also deserves an explanation. I am of course using "purdy" instead of "pretty." I do this not to be folksy, but to

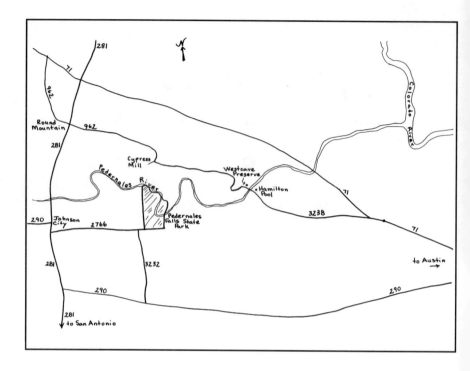

point out the incorrect but accepted pronunciation of "Pedernales." Derived from the Spanish word for flint, Pedernales has been twangified to rhyme with "burden Alice." Don't bother to look up "twangify" in the dictionary. Twangify isn't there. I made up that word.

If you are a grown-up, and you have been paying attention, you have come to understand that you can't go back home again. Each failed attempt leaves you more skeptical, and, although you haven't quit trying, you have quit crossing your fingers.

So it was with me and **Hamilton Pool.** When I took my children there in 1993, it had been nearly thirty years since I had been to Hamilton Pool. I was prepared for another scrape of the old saw. As we negotiated the steep, rocky, quarter-mile trail to the pool, I expected to see a dried-up, scum-crusted cesspool filled with beer cans and old tires. I was joyously mistaken. Hamilton Pool was even more enchanting than I had remembered. I wasn't exactly going home again, but I was in the right neighborhood.

Hamilton Pool was formed thousands of years ago when the ceiling of an underground river toppled down. What was once the roof now lies in tilted slabs at the edge of the pool, in the shade of limestone overhangs. Called a grotto, this cave-like formation of rock creates a sheltered, muffled place to swim and rest. These features did not escape the attention of Andrew J. Hamilton, tenth governor of Texas, who came here to reconstruct his thoughts and after whom the pool and the feeding creek are named.

The water of Hamilton Pool is peridot-green with mildly curious catfish lazing along the sand and gravel bottom. A crescent of sandy beach and a wading area are on the outflowing-creek side of the pool. The best part of the pool is its source-a sixty-foot waterfall that splinters on a slippery, rounded rock or, if you happen to be sitting on the rock, on your head. Sitting there, under the waterfall, all you can hear is its restful roar.

Hamilton Pool is located on FM Road 3238, 30 miles west of Austin and 90 miles northeast of San Antonio. From Austin, take State Highway 71 West just past Bee Cave and turn left (southwest) on FM Road 3238. The entrance to the park is 13 miles on the right. From San Antonio, take U.S. Highway 281 North to Round Mountain and turn right (east) on FM Road 962, just past the Exxon station. This is the road to Cypress Mill. After 7 miles, there is a Y in the road. Take the left arm of the Y, heading toward Bee Cave. The entrance to the park is 8 miles on the left. At some point along the way, FM 962 turns into FM 3238, which is also known as Hamilton Pool Road. (You will also pass by the entrance to Westcave Preserve; see later in this section.)

Hamilton Pool is a Travis County park, with park rangers and a list of no-nos: no pets, no glass, no fires, no fishing, no collecting, and no noisiness. There are also no lifeguards on duty. It is open from 9 A.M. to 6 P.M. Gates are closed at 6 p.m., and if your car is inside, it stays there until 9:00 the next morning. So there. Admission is restricted to one hundred cars. According to the park ranger who was taking the modest vehicle fee, the only time that the one hundred–car limit is reached is an occasional Sunday afternoon. Even so, a phone call ahead is recommended. Above-average rain can lead to heavy runoff, high fecal coliform bacteria counts, and temporary pool closure. The park is closed on Thanksgiving Day, Christmas Day, and New Year's Day. For information, call (512) 264-2740.

Hamilton Pool, Johnson City

If you don't want to swim or get beaten into submersion by the waterfall, or if the weather is too cool, you can go hiking. A three-quarter–mile hiking trail leads along the southern bank of Hamilton Creek from the pool to a small sandy beach on the Pedernales River. Craggy, tilted slabs of fossil-filled limestone line the banks of the creek. The hike is especially colorful in the fall when the bald cypress trees that line the creek are turning to rust. Guided nature tours are conducted on the weekends. Call the park at (512) 264-2740 for information about the hikes.

Compost toilets are available at the parking lot and a chemical toilet is available on the hiking trail about fifty yards from the pool. There are no drinking water or concessions at Hamilton Pool Park.

The entrance to **Westcave Preserve** is down the road and across the river from the entrance to Hamilton Pool—Hamilton Pool is on the east side of the Pedernales River, and Westcave Preserve is on the west side of the Pedernales River. The low-water bridge over the river is called Hammett's Crossing. The last hundred-year flood was in

1952. The Pedernales crested at seventy feet at Hammett's Crossing. Although we are not due for another flood of that volume for a while yet, it is prudent to be heedful when approaching a low-water crossing of the Pedernales River (or any river, especially one in the Hill Country) after a heavy rain. This includes Hammett's Crossing. Flashy doesn't mean snazzy when you're talking about a Hill Country river.

Like Hamilton Pool, Westcave Preserve is a grotto. It was formed when the softer layers of sand and shale underlying the harder Cow Creek limestone were washed away and the roof fell in. Spring water continued to flow from the porous limestone, depositing calcium-carbonate on the walls and tumbled-down boulders. The intricate result of this flowstone and dripstone accumulation is one of the prettiest places in the Hill Country. My snapshots hardly do it justice. That is a statement, not an apology.

This is as good a place as another to digress and talk about the photographs in this book. I once attended a one-day seminar led by Carol Barrington, an award-winning travel writer and photographer. The course blurb said that participants could bring up to ten of their own travel slides for Ms. Barrington to critique.

Eager students that we were, we all brought our best pictures and, oh, they were magnificent: mist-shrouded mountains in Tibet, grimacing aborigines at a corroboree, exotic Spanish tango dancers, smashing waves on the Scotland coast, thunderclouds framed by Gothic arches. Ms. Barrington offered hints about lighting and composition, but was thrilled, as we all were, by these evocative photographs. Then it came my turn.

I had brought my slides of Goliad, Texas. An embarrassed silence settled over the room. As she flipped through my slides, Ms. Barrington blurted out a few questions like, "What is that?" and "What were you trying to show with this photograph?" When she reached the last slide, she turned to me, forced a smile, and said, "Well, you have a good eye." I took that to mean that most of my photographs were in focus.

That sad but true story is in preface to saying that I am not a photographer. I take snapshots, and because all I have is a good eye, the most you can expect is that they are in focus. I did the best I could with the picture of Westcave Preserve, but you must visit it in order to

Bald cypress and ferns, Westcave Preserve

know that "prettiest place in the Hill Country" is not a breathy cliché.

For thousands of years, humans with varying degrees of intellectual bestowal have visited the area now called Westcave Preserve. By 1974 some of those on the lower end of the noodle scale had turned it into a garbage dump.

Enter, John F. Ahrns. With what might be perceived as a mystical sense of the area's potential and what actually was hard work, he came, he saw, and he conquered the neglect that had all but ruined Westcave Preserve. His efforts—at times, stubbornness—have earned him folk hero status among naturalists and environmentalists over the past two decades.

As you follow Mr. Ahrns or one of the other guides down the steep, cable-girded path to the grotto, the air becomes cooler and more humid. The vegetation shifts abruptly from the typical Hill Country prickly pear cactus and ashe juniper to ferns and bald cypress trees. Some of the bald cypress trees are between 400 and 600 years old, indicating that the water source has been constant. The umbrella effect of the canyon creates favorable growing conditions for about 400 species of plants and 25 species of trees. You can also see mushrooms and frogs and an occasional red dragonfly that Mr. Ahrns told me the name of but that I neglected to write down because I was so startled.

As you approach the floor of the grotto, you hear splashing water, whose sound is magnified by the canyon walls. The source of the splashing is a semicircular waterfall which is a smaller but mossier version of the Hamilton Pool waterfall. Westcave Preserve's waterfall is generated from spring water coming from porous limestone and forms an eleven-foot-deep pool. Swimming is not permitted, but you can sit on benches beside the pool as long as you like. Mr. Ahrns understands the drawing power of this place and lets you return hike at your leisure.

Since 1974 John Ahrns has reclaimed the natural beauty of Westcave Preserve. Maintaining that condition is a running battle. Limited access to the preserve, volunteer efforts, and contributions are essential for Westcave's survival. Private donations are the only source of operating funds, which means that a wolf is forever prowling at the front gate. Despite this threat, Mr. Ahrns refuses to give up. He has devoted most of his adult life to this little wrinkle on the planet, and he never intends to return it to those that would make it a garbage dump.

Westcave Preserve is open to the public on Saturdays and Sundays. Guided tours are at 10 A.M., noon, 2 P.M., and 4 P.M. Tours are limited to the first thirty people lined up at the gate. No reservations accepted. Special arrangements for weekday tours can be made for schools and other organizations. *Always, always call ahead,* especially if it has been raining, since tours are canceled if the trail is too wet. There is no charge for the weekend tours, but donations are gratefully accepted. A little donation box is at the trailhead. If you would like to become a Westcave Preserve patron, an information sheet is at the interpretive exhibit shed. If you would like to use the bathroom, there is a compost toilet adjacent to the parking area. If you would like a Big Red or a Coke, bring your own.

The mailing address is Westcave Preserve, General Delivery, Round Mountain, Texas 78663. The phone number is (210) 825-3442.

The third jewel in the Pedernales crown is **Pedernales Falls State Park,** a 4800-acre block of the Edwards Plateau, incised by the

Pedernales River and its feeder creeks. The entrance to the park is at the northeast corner of a square formed by U.S. Highways 290 and 281 and State Roads 2766 and 3232, 9 miles due east of Johnson City. It is 70 miles from the Alamo and 40 miles from the Capitol.

Pedernales Falls upstages the rest of the park and can be viewed from two scenic overlooks. One of our visits to the park was shortly after the record-breaking rains in December, 1991. Good grief. I will never stand there and argue with the park regulations that prohibit swimming along the 3-mile stretch of the Pedernales River at the park's northern edge. I've never been to Niagara Falls, but if they are anything like Pedernales Falls after a wet spell, I see why such a hoopla is made over daredevils riding barrels over them.

When the river is at its usual (as in non-flood) level, the falls area is a safe place to hike and play. Steps lead from the observation area to the river. (If the river is at flood level, the steps are closed.) The limestone river channel is slanted and stair-stepped, and evidence of the gouging action of water is everywhere—the configuration of the riverbed is like rough cut building blocks, separated by sandbars and slices of river.

Swimming, wading, and tubing are permitted downriver from the falls. A sandy beach for swimmers and tubers is about a quarter-mile from the picnic area. (Maps are available at park headquarters.) There are no lifeguards on duty, but there is an automatic early flood warning system. As mentioned previously, the Pedernales River is notoriously flashy, and if the warning siren sounds, you need to head for higher ground. Immediately. Right then. *Pronto. Mach scnell. Andale.* Despite this contingency, when confined to its banks, the Pedernales River is one of the finest swimming spots in the Hill Country.

Pedernales Falls State Park has about 15 miles of developed hiking trails calling for varying degrees of stamina. The more difficult trails require that your leg muscles go "boink, boink" when you poke them. My leg muscles go "squish, squish," so I can't tell you much about those trails; however, detailed hiking maps are available at park headquarters.

My family's favorite hike at Pedernales Falls State Park is the quarter-mile Hill Country Nature Trail that originates in the camping area between campsites 218 and 221. The trail descends into a canyon populated by a diversity of tree species: sycamore, American elm, ash, hickory, scarlet buckeye, agarito, Texas mountain laurel, persimmon, and, of course, the ubiquitous ashe juniper, mesquite, and live oak.

One of my all-time favorite trees is the Mexican buckeye (*Ungnadia speciosa*), which blooms in the spring with sweet-smelling, delicate pink flowers and in the fall with golden leaves. Best of all, it has fruits with three one-eyed seeds that are about the size and consistency of marbles. These seeds are perfect for tossing at the back of the head of the hiker in front of you.

Near the midpoint of the Hill Country Hiking Trail is a wooden deck overlooking Twin Falls—a place where two creeks join hands before plunging into the Pedernales River. This area is ecologically sensitive and is closed to foot traffic. A trail booklet describing the vegetation and ecology of the Hill Country Hiking Trail is available at park headquarters. Guided nature hikes are offered on many Saturday mornings, and bird walks are conducted on some Sunday mornings. For information about these activities, call Pedernales Falls Park Headquarters at (210) 868-7304 between 8 A.M. and 5 P.M., or write Park Superintendent, Route One, Box 450, Johnson City, Texas 78636. The usual state park admission fees are charged, and, as always, a Texas Conservation Passport lets you sail on through the gates (see Appendix 1). Please remember that this state park may close on weekdays during the winter for seasonal wildlife pruning, so always call ahead.

Pedernales Falls State Park has sixty-seven campsites and a youth-only sponsored group campsite. Designated primitive campsites are along one of the hiking trails, about 2 miles from park headquarters. Reservations for campsites are necessary. This is a very popular park. When you visit, you will understand why. For reservations call (512) 389-8900 (see Appendix 1).

Meanwhile, back in Johnson City, you can get a bowl of Steve's Industrial Strength Chili at **Hill Country Cupboard,** located at the junction of U.S. Highways 281 and 290 West. Also on the menu are sandwiches, soup, barbecue, chicken-fried steak, chicken strips, and desserts. There is a vegetable plate with four choices. Hill Country Cupboard is open every day except Christmas and New Years from 11 A.M. until 9 P.M. Call (210) 868-4625. $$

Llano and Gillespie Counties
Enchanted by the Rock

The choice is yours to make
Time is yours to take
Some sail upon the sea
Some toil upon the stone.
—Townes Van Zandt, "To Live Is to Fly"

By observing my sister, a reader of travel books, I have concluded that this chapter will determine the commercial viability of my book. At the bookstore she plucks a book from the shelf, scans the table of contents, spies a chapter she knows something about, peruses it for a minute or two to determine if the author knows diddlysquat, and either heads to the cash register or scrunches the book back onto the shelf.

Since Enchanted Rock State Natural Area near Fredericksburg is a household name, if not a mecca, to many Texans, this chapter may be the only one a prospective book buyer evaluates. That is not fair. This chapter is okay, but, after all, it is about a big old rock.

At the risk of a rocky start, I must mention that Enchanted Rock State Natural Area straddles the dotted line that divides Gillespie and Llano counties. Enchanted Rock is closer to Fredericksburg (population 7,256) than Llano (population 2,990) but contains more Llano County than Gillespie County. Among people who are proud to claim Enchanted Rock as their own, these are sensitive issues.

Enchanted Rock State Natural Area is a 1,643-acre park on Ranch Road 965, 18 miles northwest of Fredericksburg and 22 miles south-

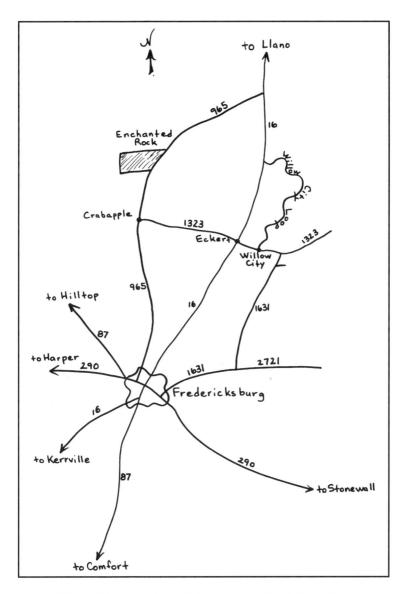

west of Llano. It is a popular park loomed over by pink, peeling domes of granite.

Enchanted Rock and its nearby companions, Little Rock, Turkey Peak, Freshman Mountain, and Buzzard's Roost, are exposed blips on the surface of a 90-square mile, billion-year-old batholith. A batholith is an incredible hunk of underground igneous rock which forms when molten rock wells up and cools. Like most batholiths, Enchanted Rock Batholith is made of granite, in its case, a coarse-grained, pink stone called Town Mountain granite. This type of granite is quarried for building stone, especially cornerstones, monuments, and tombstones. A similar pink granite from nearby Marble Falls was used to build the state capitol.

Enchanted Rock itself is near the bottom of the 15-mile-long teardrop-shaped Enchanted Rock Batholith. A combination of shoving up and washing off (uplifting and erosion) exposed the granite to the surface between fifteen and fifty million years ago, and relatively recently—say, a million or two years ago—weathering whittled it into its present, distinctive contour. Enchanted Rock is an exfoliation dome, meaning that the granite swells a little as the overlying rock erodes away and its outer layer splits and slides off. I guess you could say that this is an example of cracking up after being under too much pressure. Or, the big slabs of rock that have split away from the main rock have become disenchanted.

All this uplifting, erosion, splitting, and tumbling has left us with a unique place to ponder the vastness of time, marvel at Nature's beauty, and play hide-and-seek. The summit of Enchanted Rock is also the best spot in the whole state to fly a kite.

During these various activities on the rock, care must be taken to sidestep the vernal pools. These are weather-carved bowls of life in the granite's surface that fill with water when it rains. They provide a welcome but fragile place for plants to grow. The largest of these vernal pools, which are also called weathering pans, is on the summit of Enchanted Rock. Some of these built-in plant saucers are bare, but if we leave them alone they may eventually leaf out. Dogs that like to mark their territory need to be redirected.

Enchanted Rock State Natural Area has 8 miles of main trails and access trails. The 0.6-mile trail leading to the top of Enchanted Rock is called **Summit Trail** and takes about an hour to hike. On the way to the top, you will pass piles of exfoliated rock slabs, some of which have been weather-shaped into pedestals. The dome is also stomping ground to snakes, birds, squirrels, and lizards, like the crevice spiny lizard (*Sceloporus poinsettii*). Over five hundred plant species eke out a living in the area, and two wildflower species, the Texas bluebell

Enchanted Rock, seen from Loop Trail

(*Campanula reverchonii*) and the granite spiderwort (*Tradescantia pedicellata*), grow only in the granite-derived soils of the Llano Uplift.

Your perk at the peak is a 360-degree view of the countryside from an elevation of 1,825 feet. To the southwest is Little Rock which appears to be coming apart at the seams. To the east are Turkey Peak, Freshman Mountain, and farther off, Buzzard's Roost. If you continue over the dome toward the northwest, you will come upon one of the numerous entrances to Enchanted Rock Cave, some of which have trail markers. Near the cave entrances there is enough light to proceed for a short distance; however, further exploration of the cave—a big rock pile, really—requires a flashlight, hiking shoes, good balance, and a total absence of claustrophobia. Since I am only half-equipped to go into the cave, you will have to see it for yourself. I have never gone in, nor do I ever intend to.

Other main trails include a 4-mile **Loop Trail** which encircles the bases of Enchanted Rock, Little Rock, Freshman Mountain, and Turkey Peak, and, for a distance, follows beside Sandy Creek and **Echo Canyon Trail,** a 1-mile link between the Loop Trail and the Summit Trail.

The Loop Trail takes a moderately-conditioned family about four

Collared lizard, Enchanted Rock

hours to hike. Because of the great number and variety of birds, the same trail will take a birder all day. If you have ever tried to hike with an avid birder, you will know what I am talking about. The birder will suddenly freeze, snap binoculars into position, gaze for a few seconds with mouth agape, and triumphantly announce the name of the discovery. The birder may or may not pull out a notebook and scribble in it. Having a meaningful conversation is hopeless, since a bird sighting erases all thoughts in progress. It becomes tiresome answering the question, "Now, what were you saying?"

Sandy Creek on the Loop Trail is an excellent place to see woodpeckers, scissor-tailed flycatchers, mockingbirds, roadrunners, swallows, hummingbirds, and cardinals. The bird that my kids and husband still talk about is the painted bunting (*Passerina ciris*), a bright red, green, and blue bird about the size of a house finch. We watched one taking a bath in Sandy Creek, oblivious to the wows of his flightless, drab observers.

My son's favorite parts of the Loop Trail were an outcropping of white quartz (which he could not take a piece of because it is against park rules to do so) and a band of baby armadillos (which he could not pet because it is against his mother's rules to do so.)

There are numerous access trails that splay off the Loop Trail. Some go to primitive camping areas or scenic overlooks. Other access trails cut between Enchanted Rock and Turkey Peak and Freshman Mountain. You don't need to be too concerned if you stray off the main trail. It is hard to get lost with a big rock as a point of reference. Also, little wooden markers with arrows point the way on the Loop Trail and you-are-here maps dot the trail. There are two compost toilets on the trail, but no water, so carry a canteen if the weather dictates.

Echo Canyon Trail cuts off the Loop Trail at about the halfway point and after .5 miles joins the Summit Trail midway to the summit. The Echo Canyon Trail leads over rocks that have slid off the sides of Enchanted Rock and Little Rock. It is a very rocky trail and might be too challenging for some children and adults. If this is the case, you need not detour through the detritus of Echo Canyon, but continue around the Loop Trail. The Echo Canyon Trail is the best bivouac area if you want to watch those who seek a more exhilarating outdoor experience—rock climbers and rappelers who tackle the northwest face of Enchanted Rock.

Trail maps are available at park headquarters.

The best seasons to visit Enchanted Rock are spring and fall. Winter is okay, if there is no ice. Summer is okay if you are part lizard. It gets hot on the rock.

The entrance fee is the standard state park admission price and, as usual, Texas Conservation Passport holders are admitted free. If you still haven't gotten your Passport, turn to Appendix 1 for the whole story. There are additional fees and reservation requirements for overnight stays in one of the 166 tent camping sites, primitive backpacking sites, and primitive areas. This is one of the state's most popular parks, so make your reservations early by calling (512) 389-8900.

Rest rooms and drinking fountains are at park headquarters, in the tent camping area, and in the picnic area. There are no restaurants or vending machines, so take a picnic lunch, unless you are a dieter and skip meals.

An interpretive exhibit about Enchanted Rock is at park headquarters. For more information about Enchanted Rock State Natural Area, contact the Park Superintendent at Route 4, Box 170, Fredericksburg, Texas 78624, or call any day between 8 A.M. and 5 P.M.

at (915) 247-3903. A phone call should precede a weekday winter visit, since a seasonal rock clearing (otherwise known as a public hunt) may be underway.

My son is fearless and courageous—there is a difference—so I was flabbergasted when he climbed a third of the way up Enchanted Rock, sat down, and refused to go farther, stating simply, "I'm scared." His older sister—my timid, cautious child—rushed past him, reveling in the loftiness, the wind, and the space.

This is the same boy who takes downhill skiing literally—from the top of the mountain, he skis down, as in white-knuckled straight down. This is the same boy who lay still while his lip was sewn up and later his forehead was sewn up and later his broken leg was set. He held onto the saddle horn for thirty seconds while a startled horse bucked around the corral. I could go on, but my hands are getting sweaty, and my neck muscles are starting to hurt.

Yet, Enchanted Rock makes him scared. It must be the rock itself. It is so magnificent and rare that it pulls forth primitive emotions. It is an individual experience, and it can be a powerful one. He named it "scared." My daughter embraced it as an unaccustomed freedom. I describe it as a feeling of irrelevance in a dark wash of unfathomable time. Actually, the word "scared" gets pretty close.

ALONG THE WAY

A stone's throw from Enchanted Rock is the **Willow City Loop**, a 13-mile road through privately owned property. Signs along the way remind you to stay on the road, not to trespass, and to watch for cattle. It is a pretty drive through wildflowers and rock exposures, but slow going because of the narrow road and one-lane bridges. Children tend to be less impressed with roadside beauty than they should be; however, if they are pillow-slobbering in the back seat, this is a peaceful, pastoral side journey on the way back to Fredericksburg.

The loophead (as opposed to trailhead) is reached by turning left (northeast) on Ranch Road 965 as you leave the park. At the junction with State Highway 16 turn right (south), and drive 3.1 miles to the loop entrance which will be on the left-hand side of the road. The loop ends at Willow City where you turn right (west) on Ranch

Road 1323 and go 2.7 miles to the junction with State Highway 16, which takes you to Fredericksburg, 13 miles away. By then the kids will be awake and ready for some strudel and you will be wishing that you never had to go back to the city.

Fredericksburg is 18 miles south of Enchanted Rock if you travel by way of Ranch Road 965. For more information about that area, see the section on Fredericksburg.

At this point, I should be giving you directions to **Balancing Rock.** This natural wonder was a multi-ton plate of granite perfectly balanced on a slender rock pedestal. I say was, because during the weekend of April 19 and 20, 1986, some cretin displaced it with explosives. No one was ever charged with the crime; however, if the guilty person is ever found and convicted, fitting punishment for this pointless act would be breaking rocks on a chain gang in the company of the mental cripples that poisoned Treaty Oak and vandalized Cave without a Name. Why on earth would someone do something like that? Sawdust for brains!

Mountain Home
Saying "Y. O." to Exotic Animals

Oh my, momma ain't that Texas Cookin' good
Oh my, momma eat everyday if I could.
—Guy Clark, "Texas Cookin'"

The exact whereabouts of Mountain Home (population 96) probably does not leap to front and center in the mind of most readers. Nor does the location of Ingram (population 1,449), Hunt (population 708), or Camp Verde (population 123). These towns to the west and south of Kerrville (population 18,118) have among them the largest privately owned exotic game preserve in the world, the best mural on the side of a lumber store in the world, the second best Stonehenge in the world, and a history that, if not out of this world, is at least foreign to this continent. Of all the day vacations described in this book, this one is by far the most exotic.

This day trip is best in the spring and fall when the weather is milder and the animals are friskier.

The day trip package at the Schreiner family's Y. O. Ranch near Mountain Home, northwest of Kerrville, includes a two-hour bus tour of three hundred acres of Texas Hill Country full of native and exotic animals and a delicious, buffet-style lunch at the chuck wagon (the dining hall).

With few exceptions, these animals from different continents live together, if not in harmony, at least in mutual indifference toward (or befuddlement over) one another. Species represented are from North and South America, Europe, the Middle East, the Far East, Africa, and Australia. The animals at the Y. O. Ranch have at least one trait in common—they can tolerate drought. In fact, it was the big bad drought of the late 1940s and early 1950s that convinced

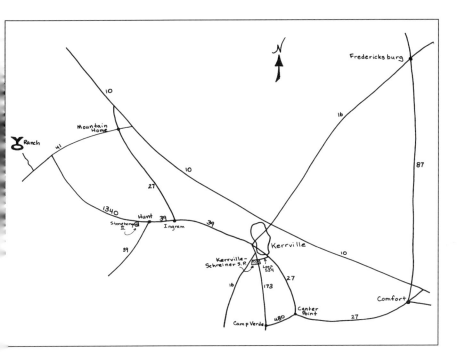

the Schreiner family to diversify. They were one of the pioneers in Texas of exotic wildlife ranching, which is now a well-established state industry.

Among the animals you might see are waterbuck, wildebeest, impala, axis deer, fallow deer, ibex, oryx, sika, eland, gazelle, zebra, elk, addax, and, best of all, giraffe. You will also see all three species of flightless birds, the emu, the rhea, and the ostrich. Don't dismiss these rather unaesthetic birds as oversized chickens. They sell for up to $60,000 per pair. Our tour guide, Jim Hanks, was unimpressed with the cerebral endeavors of one of the ranch's ostriches named Junior: "He's got a two-watt brain, but he can figure out where the corn is."

In his own way, Junior had a disarming way about him. Like many of the other animals, Junior crowded the bus for his share of the corn handout. Everyone's favorites were the magnificent giraffes, with their sticky, gray, corn-gathering tongues and huge, trusting eyes. A zoo's eye view of a giraffe gives you only a general idea how big these animals are. They are *huge*. And they are so gentle. I was able to pet one on the cheek, and one of the braver children hand-fed one. There was a baby giraffe, too.

As our tour guide pointed out animal species, he told us about their regions of origin, their behaviors, their world survival patterns, their environmental adaptations—in short, the bus tour through the Y. O. Ranch was an educational experience. Did you know, just for instance, that the Grant zebras (the ones pictured in the children's books) have to be kept in their own pastures because they are very territorial and will surround and kill intruders? Or that a zebra's stripe pattern is as unique as a human being's fingerprints? Or that a baby zebra identifies its mother by her stripes, not by her smell? I tell you, it was fascinating.

To get from the door of the Alamo to the door of the chuck wagon at the Y. O. Ranch takes every bit of two hours if you go by way of Interstate Highway 10 and State Highway 41, and if you drive the speed limit, and if you don't make any stops. That is to say, allow plenty of travel time. Reservations are required. Call (210) 640-3222.

Tours are daily at 10 A.M. and 1 P.M. Lunch for everyone—day visitors, overnight guests, ranch hands, employees, and Schreiner family members—is at noon. This means that if you have reservations for the afternoon tour, you need to arrive by noon if you intend to have lunch. This also means that your kids get to gawk at real cowboys—because of the roughness of the Hill Country terrain, the ranch's 2,000 longhorn cattle and 800 sheep are worked on horseback.

When you reach the massive front gate of the Y. O. Ranch, you are asked to phone headquarters for the combination to the lock and to relock the gate after entering. From the front gate to the chuck wagon/headquarters is another 7.4 miles on a narrow asphalt road through open, animal-inhabited pastures. Signs ask you to observe a thirty-five–mph speed limit. After I learned their prices, I understood the advisability of not hurting one of the Y. O. stock. I think it would be clever to have a sign saying, "If you don't brake, you pay." However, such a sign would not be in keeping with the friendly, low-key attitude at the ranch.

Tickets are purchased at the chuck wagon/headquarters and are less than the cost of a theme park admission ticket. The price includes lunch. While you wait for the tour to begin, you can have a complimentary cup of coffee or glass of iced tea and wander around the chuck wagon taking inventory of the required items on a chuck wagon wall:

Camp Verde General Store

family photographs, framed Ace Reid cartoons, barbed wire collec-
tions, stuffed animal heads, framed arrowheads, more stuffed animal
heads, and coat hooks made of horseshoes. The only required item
that was missing was a picture made of rattlesnake rattlers. And, truth
told, the framed arrowheads were not in the dining room but were in
the Y. O. Ranch General Store just off the dining room.

In addition to bus tours to see the exotic animals, the Y. O. Ranch
offers overnight accommodations, longhorn roundups for city slick-
ers, and environmental education camps for children. For information about overnight stays call (210) 640-3222 or write Y. O. Ranch,
Mountain Home, Texas 78058. For information about yee-haw
cowboying and summer camp, call (210) 640-3348 or write Y. O.
Ranch Adventure Camp, P.O. Box 1169, Ingram, Texas 78025.

The Y. O. Ranch was established in 1880 by Capt. Charles
Schreiner with profits from a longhorn cattle drive. His grandson
Charles Schreiner III and four great-grandsons, one of whom is
Charles Schreiner IV, continue to oversee the 45,000-acre working

ranch in the Texas Hill Country. The great-grandsons, in their thirties and forties, divide the chores: one takes care of the ranch's longhorn herd, another oversees the exotic animals, another tends to the guests, and the last is involved in marketing. I overheard someone say, "They work right along with the rest of us. None of them boys has taken to wearing gold chains and driving a Mercedes."

ALONG THE WAY

Camp Verde General Store and Post Office is across the road from the second best roadside park in the state. Picnic tables and bald cypress trees and rocks to skip are on the banks of Verde Creek, a tributary of the Guadalupe River.

(The best roadside park in the state is no longer open to the public. It is almost underneath High Bridge on the Pecos River, off U.S. Highway 90. Abandoned and crumbling, it is one of those places that lizards rule.)

But back to Camp Verde. If you are unfamiliar with Camp Verde's pre–Civil War history, a visit to the Camp Verde General Store will be puzzling. Mixed with the usual country crafts, wind chimes, books about Texas, jewelry, hard candy in jars, refrigerator magnets, quilts, toys, kitchenware, and ice cube trays that make cubes in the shape of Texas (that I bought two of and use for special occasions), there are a number of items with a camel motif. That is because Camp Verde was the site of the U.S. War Department's partially successful, but ill-timed (because of the Civil War) camel experiment.

In 1856 about eighty camels and several camel herders were imported from where camels and camel herders come from—North Africa and Asia, or thereabouts. The experiments tested the "camels' utility in the pursuit of Indians and the transportation of burdens." The curious beasts proved somewhat contrary but were better than mules for carrying heavy loads across the desert. The Civil War spoiled the camel experiment. It spoiled other things, too, dearer than camels. The camels were set free and wandered around this part of the state for a couple of decades. I wonder what the Comanches thought about them.

Still, though, the story of the camel experiment in Texas was outlandish enough to qualify for a Ripley's feature.

Camp Verde General Store has a front porch with a bench and a sweet dog named Precious. Walk with a firm step on the porch to let Precious know you're approaching so you won't startle her. She's deaf. I noticed that she watched my face more closely than most dogs do. I don't usually remember much about friendly porch dogs, but Precious was different. I smile as I remember her.

Camp Verde General Store and Post Office are 11 miles south of Kerrville at the junction of State Road 480 and State Highway 173. Write to P.O. Box 69, Camp Verde, Texas 78010, or call (210) 634-7722 for more information. Open Monday through Saturday, 9 A.M. to 5:30 P.M. and Sunday, 1 P.M. to 5:30 P.M. Smile at Precious for me.

Kerrville-Schreiner State Park is a 517-acre park on the shores of the Guadalupe River. It is located at the southern corner of Kerrville on State Highway 173, near the junction of Loop 534 (see map of Mountain Home/Y.O. Ranch) and State Highway 27. It has tent campsites, multiuse sites, trailer campsites, and screened shelters. This is a popular park, so reservations for campsites are necessary. Day activities include fishing, swimming in the river (if being unable to see the bottom doesn't bother you), picnicking, and hiking. There are nearly 8 miles of hiking paths through savannah grasslands and stands of trees that are the proper size. You might even see white-tailed deer and wild turkey. Best of all, geese and ducks waddle the banks of the Guadalupe River, and they are as enjoyable to feed as their counterparts elsewhere.

Admission to Kerrville-Schreiner State Park is the customary state park fee and is free for Texas Conservation Passport holders. For information about Kerrville-Schreiner State Park, call (210) 257-5392 between 8 A.M. and 5 P.M., or write Park Superintendent, Kerrville State Recreation Area, 2385 Bandera Highway, Kerrville, Texas 78028. For camping reservations call (210) 389-8900 (see Appendix 1).

Six miles west of Kerrville on State Highway 39 is **Ingram** (population 1,449). As part of Kerrville's centennial celebration, author and artist Jack Feagan painted sixteen murals depicting the area's history on the walls of the **T. J. Moore Lumberyard** in Ingram. The lumber company has been in business since 1892 and is shown in one of the murals. The historical murals are at the junction of State Highways 39 and 27, on the right heading west. Little plaques tell what the big pictures are depicting. On down Highway 39 on the left going toward

Stonehenge II, Hunt

Hunt is the **Ingram Dam** on the Guadalupe River. In the summer, high school and college kids go dam-sliding.

Between Ingram and **Hunt** (population 708), State Highway 39 trails beside the Guadalupe River. The Hill Country around Hunt is renowned for its well-appointed summer camps for well-fixed children and well-white-tailed leases for well-heeled hunters.

Hunt's gathering spot is **The Hunt Store** located on Highway 39 in downtown Hunt, such as it is. The store part of The Store is in the front of the store and is open from 6 A.M. until 10 P.M. It carries "most things a person might want," to borrow words from the owner Bob Denson. (This includes an impressive offering of gourmet wine—this is, after all, a high-rent area.) The back part of The Store is a cafe which opens onto a covered patio and grass basketball court. In the spring, morning glories spill over the patio fence.

The cafe is open for lunch every day from 11 a.m. until 2 p.m. and is open on Wednesday evenings for steak night. During the summer, Thursday night is pizza night, catering to the area camp counselors. The lunch menu has burgers, corn dogs, sandwiches, and an item called a French taco. This is best described as a cheeseburger minus the bun plus two flour tortillas with taco sauce on the side. It sounds strange but is actually very good. There are also daily specials, including chef salad or a smoked turkey sandwich.

The walls of The Store have the requisite number of stuffed animal heads, steer skulls, beer signs, saddles, and, of course, a picture of John Wayne. Hanging over the wine section is the best item of all—a huge hornets' nest. It was found in East Texas by a friend of the owner. It's worth stopping at The Store just to see it. Write to The Hunt Store, P.O. Box 274, Hunt, Texas 78024, or call (210) 238-4410.

At Hunt, State Highway 39 turns south and leaves the Guadalupe River. State Road 1340 takes the baton and follows the Guadalupe River for 20 miles until both play out just south of the Y. O. Ranch near the junction with State Highway 41 and State Road 1340. This is a winding but beautiful stretch of highway. When you are about 2 miles west of The Store on State Road 1340, keep your eyes peeled for **Stonehenge II**. Actually, you won't have to keep your eyes peeled at all—you round a curve and there it is. The first time I stumbled upon this stuccoed replica, I was so startled that I rearranged gravel on the side of the road.

There in the middle of a mowed field is, well, Stonehenge II. It is fashioned after Stonehenge (should I refer to it as Stonehenge I?) on the Salisbury Plain of Wiltshire, England. Stonehenge II was conceived by local residents Al Shepperd and Doug Hill and built by the latter. A replica of an Easter Island stone head is near Stonehenge II. It has on a red hat. Maybe a sombrero. I can only imagine what future archaeologists will make of Stonehenge II and a sombreroed stone head. I, for now, get a kick out of them. I've even come up with a better name—Clonehenge. Gawking is free.

Ottine
Into the Jungle at Palmetto State Park

❁

Ain't nothin' sweeter than a watermelon dream
'Cept sittin' on the front porch eatin' some peach ice cream
When life is really sweeter than it seems
That's what you've got to call a watermelon dream
—Guy Clark, "Watermelon Dream"

By some people's count, the great state of Texas has seven major eco-logical regions: West Texas desert scrub and mountain forests, Panhandle plains, North Central tall grass prairies, East Texas pineywoods, Gulf Coast sand dunes and marshes, South Texas thornbrush, and Edwards Plateau juniper-clad hills. If you were to consider Bastrop's Lost Pines as a westwardly displaced slice of East Texas, San Antonio and Austin are within a two-hour drive of five of the seven ecological regions. None of the other metropolitan areas have such accessible diversity.

Dallas and Houston can get to three regions, but bless their hearts, people living in these cities may have forgotten what undeveloped real estate looks like. People in Fort Worth can get to three regions but show little interest in land unless it is suitable for raising cattle. Odessa and Midland can also get to three ecological regions, with a bonus of the Monahans Sandhills. Corpus Christi has two regions nearby and the Gulf of Mexico thrown in for good moisture. El Paso has only one, but the Guadalupe Mountains and ski resorts are within a half-day's drive. Poor old Amarillo and Lubbock are confined to one ecological region, and it is apt to blow away. Their consolation prize is Palo Duro Canyon.

Palmetto State Park's jungle-like demeanor is an ecological square peg that does not fit into any of the major round holes. It is a bonus for South Central Texas.

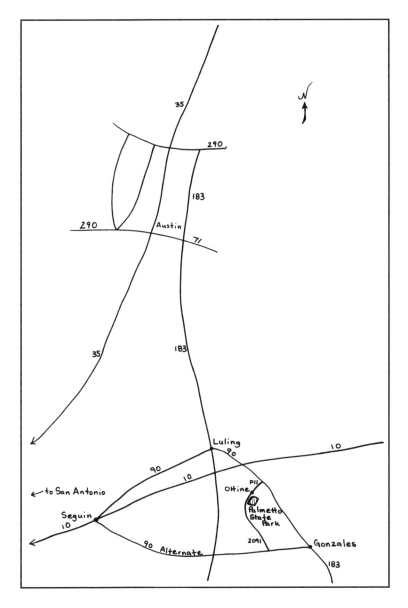

Palmetto State Park is on the banks of the San Marcos River in Ottine (population 90), a few miles south of the junction of Interstate Highway 10 and U.S. Highway 183. The park's front gate is 6 miles southeast of Luling (population 4,661) and 12 miles northwest of Gonzales (population 6,527).

As far as state parks go, Palmetto State Park is on the small end of the scale: 263 acres, 37 campsites, 2 playgrounds, 2 winky-tanks, and a little over 3 miles of developed trails. But, as far as terrariums go, Palmetto is unsurpassed. So unique are the plants that several Texas universities use Palmetto State Park as a field laboratory.

Like the canyon maples of Lost Maples State Natural Area and the loblolly pines of Bastrop State Park, the plant life at Palmetto State Park is a holdover from the Pleistocene Ice Age when the whole great state of Texas was wetter, cooler, and devoid of theme parks.

Palmetto State Park is part of the ten thousand-year old Ottine Swamp. Used to be, the fluid needs of the swamp's biota were filled by a natural warm sulfur spring and overflows of the San Marcos River. The river still overflows—on the average, once or twice a year—but the natural spring is long gone. Area farmers sucked off the shallow ground water for their own less exotic biota.

In 1936, three years after the Texas State Park Board got this swampland, a hydraulic pump was installed to sustain the sogginess. In light of the old saw about buying swampland, it would seem that the state wanted to curb wisecracks by promptly restoring the swamp condition. ("See, y'all, we *meant* to buy swampland.")

Palmetto State Park has four hiking trails, two of which have guidebooks that describe numbered trail markers. These are available at the trailheads.

The swamp-maintaining hydraulic pump is near the beginning of the one-third-mile **Palmetto Trail.** The park and this trail are named for the fan-like dwarf palmetto (*Sabal minor*). This trail has markers and a guidebook. It also has a sign warning about snakes. This is not a superfluous warning. Remember, this is a swamp. I have never seen a snake at Palmetto, but some friends of mine happened on one that refused to vacate the trail until encouraged with a well-aimed stick.

It is more likely that you will see lizards, turtles, snails, bugs, rabbits, armadillos, squirrels, and birds, lots and lots of birds. Over 240 species of birds have been recorded at the park. The commonest species are mockingbirds, cardinals, house sparrows, meadowlarks and Carolina wrens. The Carolina wren is more easily heard than seen, with its clear, sweet "chirpity, chirpity, chirpity, chirp." It is one of my favorite bird songs. A bird checklist is available at park headquarters.

Ephemeral lagoon, Palmetto State Park

The Palmetto Trail winds between ponds that are labeled "ephemeral lagoons" on the trail map. I guess that means that the ponds might dry up. Actually, in all my visits to Palmetto, I have never seen the lagoons undergo ephemeration. The mapmaker was either being obfuscatory or was covering for the eventual failure of the old hydraulic pump. In either case, I like the word "ephemeral." It makes me think of white lace curtains, billowing in the breeze.

The **River Nature Trail** also has numbered posts that correspond to the guidebook. It is a two-thirds-mile, **P**-shaped trail that follows along the sandy banks of the San Marcos River for the straight part of the **P** and through hardwood bottomlands for the curved part of the **P**. At one point in the P-walk, you will reach an apparent divergence in the road. But, unlike Robert Frost's divergence in the road, it does not make a whit of difference which one you take. Both roads are traveled by the same amount, since it is a loop trail.

The trailhead (the bottom of the **P**) is near the playground area adjacent to the park refectory, a covered group picnic area. The refectory was built in 1934 by the Civilian Conservation Corps. It is built of red rocks and looks like it is melting. I like the building, but I do not like the word "refectory." It makes me think of a humorless church deacon.

The cleverly named **Hiking Trail** is a 1.25-mile loop course that winds through hardwood bottomlands. The trail is actually a four-foot swath through hip-high grass. Curling grapevines and things that go buzz and rustle in the grass make this trail a bit menacing for some people. During warm months, mosquito repellent is necessary for all the hiking trails, but especially for the Hiking Trail. This trailhead is also near the melting red rock refectory.

The two-thirds-mile **Lake Trail** loops around the park's oxbow lake. An oxbow lake forms when a river swings too wide during high water times and then gets cut off from the mainstream during the low water times by accumulation of silt. The Lake Trail is the least interesting of the four hiking trails, unless you are a bird-watcher or turtle-watcher or you like grape vines and wildflowers. It is a smooth, flat path and only takes a jiffy to walk.

For more information about Palmetto State Park, write the Park Superintendent at Route 5, Box 201, Gonzales, Texas 78629, or call (210) 672-3266 between 8 A.M. and 5 P.M. State park admission fees apply. For campsite reservations call (512) 389-8900.

IN THE AREA

Ottine is a town nearest Palmetto State Park and is known nationwide for Warm Springs Rehabilitation Hospital. Warm Springs offers quality services for people with disabilities, including brain injuries. In 1992 Warm Springs was granted a three-year accreditation with the Commission on the Accreditation of

Texas Heroes Monument, Gonzales

Rehabilitation Facilities, the highest level of accreditation offered.

Luling is one of those long, skinny towns that hugs the railroad tracks as if its life depended on it. Its early life—rough and violent as any in Texas—depended heavily on the railroad during the late 1800s. In the 1920s an eccentric New Yorker named Edgar B. Davis discovered oil in Luling. Oil was not discovered near Luling. It was discovered *in* Luling. Over one hundred pumpjacks still tip their horseheads up and down within the city limits. One is right behind the Dairy Queen. Others scattered about town are rigged up like a butterfly, a girl eating a watermelon, and the like. Tony the Tiger is in Alfred Pope's backyard. Asked if the whine of the polishing rod and whir of the motor kept him awake, he said he's used to it.

If you have ever lived in West Texas where pumpjacks are massive, majestic, and moving proof of a good gamble, a little pumpjack dressed up like Spuds MacKenzie riding a surfboard is embarrassing. I can only imagine the colorful verbiage a veteran roughneck would offer about this parody.

Luling is thumping along, though. The movie theater has shut down, but a block down the street is the video rental store. The old building that once housed the roller-skating rink is now a karate school. The Dairy Queen still rules—no golden arches yet.

Luling's annual doo-dah is the Watermelon Thump, held the last Thursday through Sunday in June. Watermelon-eating and seed-spitting contests are the big crowd pleasers. The Thump office is in downtown Luling by the railroad tracks, naturally. For Thump information contact the Luling Chamber of Commerce, 308 North Magnolia, P.O. Box 710, Luling, Texas 78648, or call (210) 875-3214.

Luling City Market, by the railroad tracks, is a barbecue place where steaming, sauced-up meat is served on butcher paper. The usual suspects are rounded up for side dishes: beans, potato salad, sliced bread, and beer. Places like this are why I make a practice of taking along a sopping wet washrag in a plastic bag when I go on day vacations. If you do not have a washrag, there is a sink to wash your hands in the dining room. For big cleanup jobs, there is a water hose out back. Luling City Market is open Monday through Saturday, 7 A.M. to 6 P.M. Closed Sunday. Bring cash, but not much. Call (210) 875-9019. $

Natal's Produce and Nursery is by the railroad tracks in Luling at the intersection of U.S. Highway 183 and State Highway 90. It is a family-owned and operated, open-year-round, always-have-fresh-tomatoes place. They are open every day from 8 A.M. until the sun goes down. Call them at (210) 875-9028.

In the other direction down U.S. Highway 183 is **Gonzales,** a town with a proud and abundant history—only Austin and San Antonio have more historical markers. The Chamber of Commerce will provide a key to a self-guided driving tour. Children hate self-guided driving tours. So do I.

The first shots of the Texas Revolution were fired near Gonzales in October, 1835, when a Mexican army patrol from San Antonio tried to retrieve a six-pound cannon in the possession of the Texas settlers. The cannon had been loaned to the settlers for protection against Indians, but the original owners wanted it back when the Mexican subjects started acting like a bunch of unruly Texans.

Hoisting a flag that would do proud any card-carrying member of the National Rifle Association, the Texas settlers fired on the Mexican militia. The flag with the picture of a cannon and the words "Come and Take It," and, more importantly, the sass it showed, are treasured pieces of Texas history. This incident is right up there with Travis drawing the line in the dirt at the Alamo and Roger Staubach's Hail Mary pass to Drew Pearson that cinched the 1975 NFL division play-off game against the Minnesota Vikings.

I have no argument with hallowed history, but I would like to share some thoughts about the flag incident. Perhaps the Mexican commander did not perceive it as a dare, just an abbreviated version of, "Why don't y'all come and take it." It is doubtful that the Mexican army ever saw the flag. The fog on that October morning in 1835 was as thick as split frijole soup. It does not really matter, though. The Revolution had begun.

The settlers in Gonzales were the ones credited with starting the Texas Revolution, and they were the only settlers who answered Travis's pleadings for reinforcements during the Alamo siege. The **Texas Heroes Monument** honors these thirty-two men who were killed in action at the Alamo. If it is not on your way, I would not make a special trip to Gonzales. Children couldn't generally care less about historically significant places. Besides, somebody needs to weed and water the grass around the monument.

Pleasanton
A Playground Worth a Thousand Dreams

✴

I'm gonna build me a boat with these two hands
It'll be a fair curve from a noble plan
Let the chips fall where they will
Cause I've got boats to build
—Guy Clark and Verlon Thompson, "Boats to Build"

Pleasanton (population 8,042) is a pleasant town 40 miles south of the Alamo. There, on the banks of the Atascosa River, is a playground built of wood, metal, rubber tires, sand, and dreams.

This day trip is for families that have one or more children in the age range that I call the can-I-have-one-more-kiss-goodnight years. There are also the will-you-read-me-a-story years, the can-I-have-a-snow-cone years, and the will-you-ride-on-the-ferris-wheel-with-me years. They are the best years in all eternity, those years.

I rarely recommend an interstate highway if a state highway or a U.S. highway will land you in the same spot, but in this instance I feel I must. U.S. Highway 281 to Pleasanton is my notion of what Erskine Caldwell's *Tobacco Road* looks like—junkyards, ratty houses, rusting cars, and rotting tires. In comparison, Interstate Highway 37 to the State Highway 97 cut-off to Pleasanton is a boulevard.

Pleasanton was once the county seat of Atascosa County. In 1910 a county seat election was called, and nearby Jourdanton (population 3,374) took the prize. For a while, Pleasanton chose to retain the court records. During a Saturday night dance in Pleasanton, the records were relocated to Jourdanton. The records were not exactly stolen, seeing as how Jourdanton had been voted the rightful custodians; however, this wrestling match did little for the solidification of brotherhood between the two towns. (I say brotherhood rather

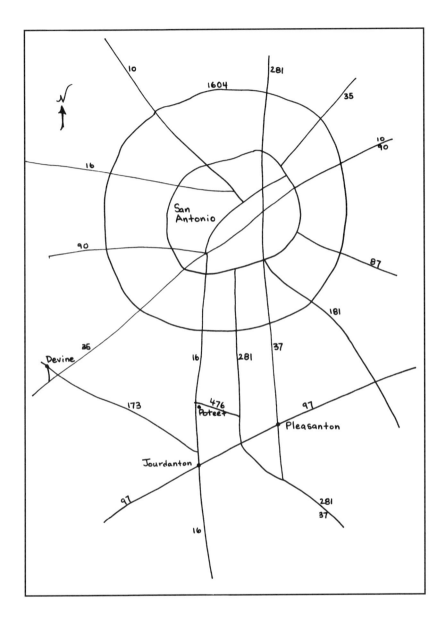

than sisterhood because sisters would have declared themselves co-county seats and a built a courthouse halfway between the two towns.)

Undaunted, Pleasanton declared itself the "Birthplace of the Cow-boy." Jourdanton—and, for that matter, any town in the area—could have staked the claim as legitimately as Pleasanton, but it was

Pleasanton that first whipped up the idea. To punctuate the coup, they erected a bronze statue in front of their city hall. Pleasanton and Jourdanton continue to share an invigorating rivalry; however, if a joint effort is necessary, sparring ceases. Such was the necessity in 1987 when a playground needed to be planned, funded, and built. It happened, this joint effort, and the way that it happened is a story that I enjoy telling.

Once upon a time in 1986, Kyle Peeler, an attorney from Pleasanton, was thumbing through a copy of *Smithsonian* magazine as he waited for his appointment with the optometrist. He noticed an article about a man named Robert Leathers who designed playgrounds. Since Kyle had overheard his wife Pam and some of her friends discussing the community's need for a quality playground for their small children, he mentioned the article to her.

Pam talked to her friend Rachel Hurley, and they decided that they had nothing to lose by contacting this man from New York, this Robert Leathers fellow. Within a few weeks, they received a letter from Mr. Leathers giving a brief, general overview of his approach to building playgrounds.

Rachel and Pam brought up the idea at the next meeting of the Chamber of Commerce auxiliary. As Rachel put it, "We didn't know any better, so we decided to do it. Even though we were in the middle of the oil slump, we felt we could get the community behind us on this thing." As it turned out, they were right.

The deposit was sent and Mr. Leathers told a small town in South Texas how to build a playground. He told them which committes to form (twelve in all) and the precise responsibilities of each, the tools and materials that would be needed, suggestions for obtaining donations, the construction schedule, the cost breakdown of playground components, even how to label tools. Early on, the Pleasanton elementary school students were asked what they wanted in their playground.

Nearly every citizen in Pleasanton was personally contacted by telephone by Pleasanton High School D.E.C.A. (Distributive Education Clubs of America) students and offered the chance to contribute or participate. Cochairpersons Rachel Hurley and Pam Peeler spoke to any group that would listen, and most civic organizations,

Cowboy statue in front of City Hall, Pleasanton

churches, and area businesses donated money, food, or materials. Even residents of nearby Poteet helped—the owners of South Texas Distributing Company donated a prize-winning steer that they purchased at the Atascosa Livestock Show. During one week, elementary school student volunteers were stationed at the grocery stores seeking donations. The *Pleasanton Express* urged its readers: "Don't pass them by; even those few pennies that you received in change will help!"

The biggest single fundraiser was a barbecue and dance held about one month before construction was scheduled to begin. Among the raffled prizes was a Chevy S-10 Blazer, donated by the Pleasanton Chevrolet dealership. The man who won the drawing donated it back to the playground project, and with that donation, the coffers were full. It was time to build.

What began as a kitchen table dream six months earlier came true during the first five days of April in 1987. Working from 7 A.M. until 10 P.M. on some days, community volunteers were joined by building trades students from the Pleasanton junior high and high schools, a community service crew from Southwestern Bell, and airmen and airwomen stationed at Lackland Air Force Base in San Antonio. For safety reasons children were not allowed in the actual construction area; however, they were given jobs like scrubbing the rubber tires and washing bolts and screws. Power tools, hand tools, and other equipment were tagged and pooled. During the five days of construction, a single extension cord was misplaced. Pleasanton and Jourdanton Boy Scouts pitched their tents and guarded the construction area at night. Volunteers provided child care for workers' small children. Large quantities of food were prepared and served—dinner on the ground, I suppose you could call it.

In the spirit of a traditional barn raising, about two thousand people ultimately participated in the construction of the playground. This was a community effort in the old-fashioned, throat-tightening sense of the word. The result was a top-notch playground. Years later, the participants still talk about their community's accomplishment with unmistakable pride.

The playground, designed according to the wishes of the children of Pleasanton, has a dragon slide, a space platform, a boat, a maze, a balance beam on a chain, four types of bridges, a tunnel slide and a circular slide, parallel bars and chin-up bars, a sandbox, a horizontal ladder, and a tire swing. Benches, picnic tables, and an amphitheater are nearby.

The official motto for this community project was, "Build a dream for the kid in all of us." I think they did that and a lot more. I think they affirmed something for us all.

The playground is on the banks of the Atascosa River near the north end of the city's park. Entering Pleasanton via Highway 97, you will cross the railroad tracks. On the right will be a log cabin that houses the Pleasanton Chamber of Commerce. Take the first right after the Chamber and right again on Park Road which goes to City River Park.

For more information about Pleasanton, contact the Pleasanton Chamber of Commerce, 605 Second Street, P.O. Box 153, Pleasanton, Texas 78604. The phone number is (210) 569-2163. The lady answering the phone is Alice Parker, who is one of those rare and valuable people who knows the answer to all your questions. And, if she doesn't know, she can tell you who does.

IN THE AREA

Yellow spring. Spring comes to the Hill Country in a murmur of azure bluebonnets, pink evening primrose, and purple verbena. In contrast, South Texas spring arrives in a bugle of yellow. Unremarkable

Blackbrush acacia in bloom, Pleasanton

at other times of the year, the huisache and blackbrush acacia trees blaze auburn and creamy yellow during March and early April. Wild mustard, camphor weed, and yellow primrose decorate the South Texas plain. With no hills to pester it, even the sunlight is yellower. State Highway 173 runs east-west between Jourdanton and Devine; it is good yellow sun country.

The **Triple C Restaurant** on Interstate Highway 35 at Devine is an excellent, family-style restaurant specializing in steaks and seafood. The children's menu has chicken fingers, steak fingers, and chicken-fried steak. There is also a soup-and-salad bar and a grilled chicken breast. The Triple C Restaurant is open every day except Christmas. Sunday through Thursday, it is open from 6 A.M. until 10 P.M., and on Friday and Saturday, it is open from 6 A.M. until 11 P.M. Write P.O. Box 467, Devine, Texas 78016, or call 1-800-499-1501. $$-$$$

If you are intrigued by the spoils of recreational hunting, you should visit the Triple C Restaurant during deer hunting season. The parking lot is full of hunting vehicles, many of them painted camouflage. If the hunter was successful, one or more animal carcasses are prominently draped across the vehicle.

Hunting is one of those guy-things that I don't understand really, but that I harbor no ill-will toward. I love to eat venison, and, since you can't go to a supermarket and buy it, my husband has to go do his guy-thing and bring home a non-viable (as in dead) deer every year. I'm afraid that my friends who are concerned with animal rights are outnumbered by us who like to do this guy-thing and/or enjoy its spoils.

I, on the other hand, support the rights of Brussels sprouts—leave those nasty-tasting, cabbage-looking little creatures on the stalk where they can enjoy a long, bitter life before going to seed. Although they are in no danger of overpopulating and slowly starving to death unless they are seasonally thinned, I still support the rights of Brussels sprouts. And even though burgeoning populations of Brussels sprouts pose no threat to crops and soil-conserving natural vegetation, I still say leave 'em alone.

Stonewall
Looking for the Real LBJ

There's lots of people in the world today
They try to drink their cares away
But if they knew how happy they could be
They'd be asking Mama for her recipe.
—Marcia Ball, "Mama's Cooking"

In keeping with the nature of the man himself, the layout of the Lyndon B. Johnson Historical Parks is confusing. It is like this: the Lyndon B. Johnson State Historical Park and the contiguous **Ranch Unit** of the Lyndon B. Johnson National Historical Park are 5 miles east of peach-famed Stonewall (population 245) on U.S. Highway 290. The **Johnson City Unit** of the Lyndon B. Johnson National Historical Park is in Johnson City (population 959), which is 14 miles away. This part concerns the park section near Stonewall, which is what most people are referring to when they talk about visiting LBJ State Park. I'm not sure that my explanation helped clarify matters.

Anyway. The Visitor Center Complex on the grounds of the LBJ State Park houses a family album–type collection of photographs of Lyndon B. Johnson (many of them taken at his ranch), exhibits about the Hill Country, and some of the gifts that people gave Johnson while he was president. I can imagine what President Johnson said when he received a button-mosaic wall hanging depicting a horse.

The Visitor Center also has a bookstore, an auditorium for the slide show, and an information desk. It is at the information desk that you can get a park brochure, a trail map, and a poker chip for the free bus tour to the national historical park.

The only visitor access to the national historical park is by tour bus. Tours leave at regular intervals from the Visitor Center. The buses are driven—actually coaxed along—by National Park Service personnel. Each bus unit has two cabs with enough seats for fifty-five people. The buses frequently fill up—a quarter of a million people visit the park every year—explaining the business with the poker chip. You need a chip to get on the bus since the tours are first-come, first-served. The best seats in the bus are at the front of the second cab. These seats face backward and are over the tire well. If the bus is not too full, you can prop up your feet. The buses are not air-conditioned so a window seat is best in hot weather.

The tour lasts about one and a half hours. Two types of people should take the tour: (1) people who like LBJ and (2) those who don't. For the former, the script is everything you want it to be—the energy, the power, the pride, and the personality of this complex man are emphasized. The strengths of his presidency, especially his civil rights and education legislation, are underscored, and its controversial aspects are downplayed. For the latter, the tour is a chance to reconsider this native Texan in light of his beginnings.

The tour route originates at the Visitor Center, runs alongside and then crosses the Pedernales River. The first stop is the one-room schoolhouse where LBJ started school. His teacher was Miss Kate Deadrich. In 1965 Miss Deadrich and her famous pupil were reunited on the steps of this little schoolhouse. She served as his witness when he signed the Elementary and Secondary Education Act. Less than a mile away from the schoolhouse is the reconstructed birthplace house. A recorded message by Lady Bird Johnson describes, among other things, how the original house had "duh-tear-uh-ated." That is East Texas dialect for "deteriorated."

Across the road is President Johnson's final resting place. It is here, beneath huge live oak trees, in a simple family cemetery, that the thirty-sixth president is buried. In his tribute to LBJ, Cactus Pryor spoke of the president's affection for the place where he was born, where he ranched, where he conducted presidential business, and where he is buried: "He died where he most enjoyed living—at his ranch just a short distance from the waters of the Pedernales, so important to one who works the land along its banks and who draws a peace of mind from the ripples and reflections and sounds of water in a dry land."

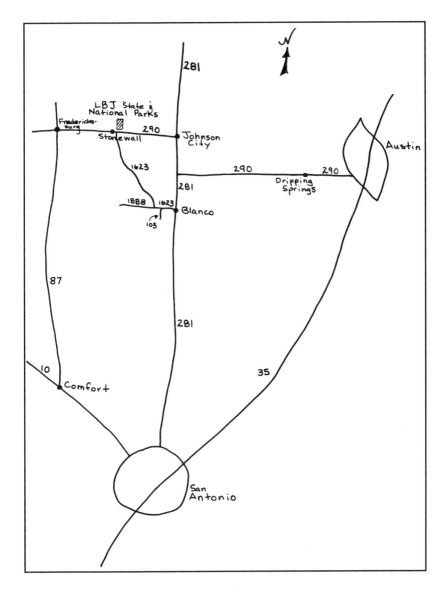

The next stop is in front of the LBJ Ranch House where Lady Bird Johnson still lives for part of the year. If Mrs. Johnson is at home, she sometimes comes out on the porch to wave at the tour buses. What a classy lady! Included in the menagerie of vehicles behind the main house are Johnson's two Lincoln Continental convertibles, a pickup truck, an amphibious car, and a fire truck.

The ranch's show barn and holding pens for the Hereford show stock are the final stops on the tour. At some level, anyway, the LBJ Ranch is still a going operation. The LBJ imprint is on the horns of the bulls. The LBJ imprint is on the land as well. During the last few miles of the tour, improved pastureland (land that, in this part of the state, may support one cow-calf pair per seven to ten acres) and un-improved pastureland (land that may support one cow-calf pair per seventeen to twenty acres) are on opposite sides of the road. They are strikingly different.

The LBJ Ranch is beautiful. It is a place that any person would be proud to show off to visitors. And its owner, the man described by Bill Porterfield as containing "an abundance of both virtue and flaw," loved it. This ranch was his place.

In the introduction to *This Place of Memory: A Texas Perspective,* Joyce Gibson Roach could have been talking about President Johnson when she described man's need for a place: "It was always knowing beyond a shadow of a doubt that one was complete, satisfied, not wanting, not needing and that even if sense of place was occasionally fleeting it served as a point of reference, of return and it was always there to call on, to summon, to sustain, and to find again."

Whether or not you liked LBJ, there is a message among the care-fully phrased lines of the brochure, the homey photographs, and the live oak trees. Lyndon B. Johnson valued these limestone hills. I be-lieve that is worth knowing.

The LBJ State Park is more than a bus stop for the LBJ National Park tour buses. It has a swimming pool, tennis courts, playgrounds, picnic areas, and a baseball diamond. A trail leads to the LBJ statue, past pens holding longhorn cattle, bison, and white-tailed deer, and to a living history farm, the **Sauer-Beckmann Farmstead.** The farm is a quarter-mile from the Visitor Center and can also be reached by car.

The Sauer-Beckmann Farmstead seeks to recreate Hill Country life as it was in the early 1900s. The day we visited was wash day. A black cast iron vat full of the week's laundry bubbled over a fire in the yard. I am not sure how the living history farm wives did their laundry.

There is some balance, functioning as it does without electricity, that the Sauer-Beckmann farm is in a park dedicated to the man whose

Johnson Family cemetery,
LBJ National Park

efforts—tireless efforts—brought electrical power to the impoverished families of the Texas Hill Country. The Pedernales Electric Cooperative, organized by Hill Country citizens and guided to fruition by a then-junior congressman born in nearby Stonewall, received a government loan through the Rural Electrification Program in 1938. But not without direct approval from President Franklin D. Roosevelt. Lyndon Johnson got that approval. A little over a year later, Hill Country residents were reading their Bibles by light bulb.

According to what day of the week and what season it is, the park employees, dressed in farm-type clothes, are doing various farm-type chores. There are even some hens laying eggs in a farm-type way. It was comforting to learn that some methods haven't changed all that much.

The main entrance to the LBJ State Park is 5 miles east of Stonewall on U.S. Highway 290. The Visitor Center is open daily from 8 A.M. to 5 P.M. (summer hours are 9 A.M. to 6 P.M.) The Sauer-Beckmann farm is open daily from 8 A.M. to 4:30 P.M. (summer hours are 9 A.M. to 5:30 P.M.). Maybe the chickens sleep late. For park headquarters, call (210) 644-2241 or 644-2252 or 868-7128. Admission for the bus tour is nominal.

ALONG THE WAY

Blanco State Park in Blanco (population 1,265) is a shore-hugging, 110-acre park on a curve in the Blanco River. It has picnic tables,

Dog-run, Sauer-Beckmann Living History Farm, LBJ State Park.

playgrounds, screened shelters, campsites, trailer pads, a walking trail, rest rooms, and, best of all, ducks to feed. This is a fine spot to pause for a Cherry Mash candy bar from the nearby Exxon station (subtitled CJ's Food Plaza). The park is open every day from 8 A.M. to 5 P.M. The entrance fee is the usual state park admission price and is waived for holders of the Texas Conservation Passport (see Appendix 1). The park is located at (and under) U.S. Highway 281 on the Blanco River. For information about Blanco State Park, call (210) 833-4333 between 8 A.M. and 5 P.M. or write Park Superintendent, Blanco State Park, Box 493, Blanco, Texas 78606. For campsite reservations, call (512) 389-8900 (see Appendix 1).

Want to see some **dinosaur tracks?** There are some in the Glen Rose limestone of the Blanco River bottom near Blanco. Turn west on Farm Road 1623 (see map) off of U.S. Highway 281. (This is on the way to Stonewall if you are coming from the direction of San Antonio.) Go 3.5 miles to Blanco County Road 103 and turn left (south). The road almost immediately crosses the Blanco River. The footprints are about fifty feet downriver from the bridge or about halfway between the bridge and a gravel bar. The prints may be partially filled or even covered with shallow water, requiring a little wading for a good look. Each footprint is about three feet long with a hindprint and foreprint. One hint: the prints have raised edges where the mud oozed up around hind and front feet. The tracks belong to a sauropod, a dinosaur that lived about 120 million years ago.

I don't know of any restaurants in Stonewall; however, the sections in this book on Fredericksburg and Johnson City mention nearby restaurants.

Vanderpool

A Maple for All Seasons

By sunup time this morning, many trees will know my name
I'll whisper to the leaves as I walk past.
—Steve Fromholz, "Jake's Song"

Lost Maples State Natural Area is a 2,208-acre park in the Hill Country which is bragged on statewide for its autumn colors. Among us guidebook naturalists, a negative response to the question, "Have you visited Lost Maples this fall?" is met with consternation. Neglecting the seasonal pilgrimage to Lost Maples near Vanderpool (population 20) is not as serious a blunder as trashing the highway, but, in some circles, it is better to change the subject than admit you missed the fall color show.

If I were Mother Nature, I would be perturbed by the following statement in the Lost Maples brochure: "To obtain information on the condition of autumn coloration before planning a visit, call the toll-free number 1-800-792-1112 after the first of October." This implies that "autumn coloration" is the sole reason for a trip to Lost Maples State Natural Area.

If weather conditions have been just right, the canyon maples (*Acer grandidentatum*) are gorgeous. Although sparser, they compare favorably with the sugar maples of Vermont; however, Texas is not Vermont. Sometimes, lots of times really, Texas has dry spells and summery autumns. These weather conditions favor starch formation in the dying maple leaves, turning them brown. Moisture, cool temperatures, and sunshine favor sugar formation. Leaves full of sugar are red which, no doubt, make for a cheerful toll-free message about the "autumn coloration."

The maple show-off weeks contribute, paradoxically, to scanty use

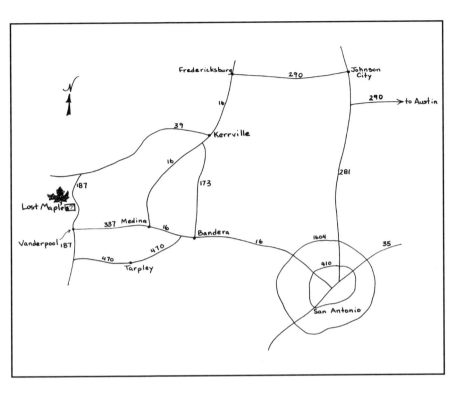

of the park at other times of the year. Prospective visitors assume that if the "autumn coloration" is average or if it is the off-season, a visit would be disappointing. This conclusion is wrong-headed. Lost Maples State Natural Area is a complex ecological niche with links to the Pleistocene Ice Age. Its distinctive features earned it a designation as a national natural landmark in 1980. A few weeks of "autumn coloration" are only part of the reason.

Interpretive exhibits at the Lost Maples park headquarters trace the westward recession of the Texas shoreline over the last one hundred million years. Scientists call our time slot the Recent Epoch of the Quaternary Period of the Cenozoic Era. "Nowadays" is easier for me to remember.

During "other days," an ice sheet covered much of North America. Regions not covered with ice were cooler and wetter than now. Species of plants flourished in areas where they otherwise would not have; however, the ice receded and with it the heat-sensitive vegetation. Traces of once-abundant American smoketree, Canada moonseed, witch-hazel, and canyon maples were cloistered in canyons, away from weather extremes. The Sabinal River canyon of Lost Maples State Natural Area is such a canyon.

These lost, stranded, if you will, maples are the flagship of this biologically diverse area, but are not the whole fleet. Several species of amphibians and fish are restricted to the Sabinal River canyon and over two hundred species of birds have been sighted. Then, there are the usual Hill Country assortment of squirrel, armadillo, javelina, raccoon, and white-tailed deer.

Winter is my favorite season to visit Lost Maples. I have all 2,208 acres, with its 10 miles of developed trails virtually to myself. There are four hiking trails: Maple Trail (0.4 mile), East Trail (4.2 miles), West Trail (3.4 miles), and a loop off the West Trail appropriately called the West Loop Trail (1.8 miles).

Spur trails off the main trails lead to primitive camping sites and scenic overlooks. Free relief maps (maps that show elevation and where to relieve yourself in composting toilets) are available at the park head-quarters. One suggestion about visiting Lost Maples in winter: the park is occasionally closed for seasonal sapling protective measures, so telephone the park headquarters before embarking.

The Maple Trail is a developed trail, well-marked and wide enough for a Suburban. Wide trails are a comfort to me when I am hiking with my children. I have a recurring, intrusive fear that I will lose one of them while hiking, only to have them turn up in Cotulla three days later, tired and hungry, but otherwise okay. Temporarily mis-placing one's child is cause for concern, but the newspaper headlines would be so awkward: Longing Mom Loses Lad in Lost Maples, Search Continues for Lost Maples Lost Little One, Child Lost in Lost Maples Found at Last in Cotulla, and so on.

But, I wander from the Maple Trail. The Maple Trail follows along the west bank of the Sabinal River, crossing it twice before merging with the East Trail. In fact, heading out on the Maple Trail and returning to the trailhead by way of the East Trail is a noisy 2-mile walk in the winter. It is noisy because of wintering song-birds, the Sabinal River over limestone rocks, and wind that twirls the maple seeds and gets tangled in steadfast sycamore leaves. The sycamores are jealous of the maples and try to prove superiority by

East Trail, Lost Maples State Nature Area

refusing to shed their leaves. Instead, the leaves cling and clamor.

On second thought, spring is my favorite season to visit Lost Maples. The eastern redbuds (*Cercis canadensis*) offer their answer to the famous fall foliage with an explosion of rose-purple flowers. They begin to bloom in late February or early March and attain full glory within a few weeks.

About the time the redbud flowers give way to leaves, the Texas mountain laurel (*Sophora secundiflora*) bloom and saturate the spring breeze with the aroma of grape Kool-Aid (that is what it smells like to me, anyway). Sophorine, a liquid alkaloid, is actually the source of the fragrance. The Texas mountain laurel, which is not really a laurel tree, but is called one anyway, has a number of vernacular names: Mescal Bean, Coral Bean, Big-drunk Bean. These names refer to the tree's red seeds, which make pretty, but poisonous, necklaces. My husband calls the seeds "burn beans." If you rub a seed against a rock, it will get hot enough to actually burn someone.

Bird-watchers and their more devoted counterparts, birders, flock (sorry, couldn't resist) to Lost Maples in April and May to see nesting golden-cheeked warblers, black-capped vireos, and green kingfishers. I understand that Lost Maples is one of the few places in the state where all three of these Texas show birds can be observed. A bird checklist, compiled by Robert F. and Judy H. Mason, is available at headquarters.

Summer is the best season of all at Lost Maples if you like to watch lizards and birds and bugs and armadillos or if you like to wade in a clear, shallow river. The baby green anoles are the most endearing. Commonly called chameleons, green anoles (*Anolis carolinensis*) are not true chameleons, although, like the latter, anoles do change color with light, temperature, and mood. As you peer at the baby anoles, they cock their little heads and stare back, the balance between curiosity and fear in your favor. Then their mama calls, I guess, and they flit away.

That is in contrast to the nearsighted armadillos that snuffle through the underbrush, and if they chance to notice you, do a startled pirouette and crash away.

And, then there is autumn and "autumn coloration."

During October and November, you may find Lost Maples a bit crowded. Let me hasten to explain what I mean by crowded in the context of Lost Maples. Crowded at Lost Maples means that you may not be able to park your car ten steps from the trailhead. Crowded means that you may have to wait a minute or two to use the public winky-tank. Crowded means you will see other hikers, backpackers, and fannypackers on the trails.

Crowded at Lost Maples does not mean waiting in line to pay an outrageous admission price and waiting in line to squeeze aboard a roller coaster and waiting in line to pay six dollars for a mediocre hamburger. It does not mean huddling with the masses in a stadium where you applaud well-trained animals yearning to breathe free while being subjected to dreadful background music.

Lost Maples–crowded is not the same as theme park-crowded; however, to avoid the crowds at Lost Maples, I have some suggestions: (1) arrive early in the day, (2) go during the week, even if it means playing hooky, because it is worth it, (3) pack a lunch and canteen and hike the family-friendly East Trail, and (4) keep "crowded" in perspective—there is enough fresh air and sunshine to go around.

Elk at Las Campanas

The East Trail requires between three and four hours for a moderately conditioned family to hike. This estimated time takes into account pauses to admire the limestone walls above the Sabinal River, the scenic overlooks and overhangs (the latter covered on their dripping undersides by maidenhair fern), ponds, and a twenty-foot waterfall on Can Creek. This also allows time to rest after the quarter-mile climb up the side of a hill. The map warns you that there is a steep area. There is, but you are rewarded with several acres of mountain laurel trees and a breezy view from the top of the Edwards Plateau.

As I considered destinations to include in this book, I asked a lot of people what they thought were the best places to go in this part of Texas. Mentioned most often and in reverent tones—even by people that I would not have guessed had naturalist leanings—were Lost Maples and Enchanted Rock. Enchanted Rock is about mountaintop experiences and its tug is easy to figure. But what defines Lost Maples?

The maple trees are spectacular. So are the flame-leaf sumacs, the sycamores, and the copper and bronze hackberries. Grasses going to seed ripple golden and purple and rust in the autumn sunlight. The sky, so often white hot in Texas, turns to a thick blue in November. All these colors are looked after by a skeleton-white canyon wall. It is not the maple trees that bring me back season in and season out. It is the feeling of being looked after. Maybe that is why the maples chose to stay.

Lost Maples State Natural Area is open every day, with the possible exception of a few days each winter, as previously mentioned. Admission is free for those with a Texas Conservation Passport (see Appendix 1) or is the usual state park admission fee for those without. Bathrooms are available at the park headquarters and near the trailhead, and compost toilets are strategically placed along the hiking trails. Drinking fountains are at headquarters and near the trailhead, but not on the trail, so carry a canteen if the weather dictates. If you want to eat anything, it would be best to pack a picnic lunch, since there are no restaurants in or near the park.

For more information, contact Park Superintendent, Lost Maples State Natural Area, HCO1, Box 156, Vanderpool, Texas 78885, or call (210) 966-3413 between 8 A.M. and 5 P.M. For campsite reservations call (512) 389-8900 (see Appendix 1).

ALONG THE WAY

Medina. What Charles Apelt of Comfort was to the armadillo and Ed and Susan Auler of Tow are to the Texas wine industry, so are Baxter and Carol Adams of Medina (population 515) to the state's fledgling apple industry. The Adams' put in their first apple orchard in 1981. A decade later they have expanded their operation to four thousand trees and in the process formed the core of a new Texas industry. Apple harvest time is celebrated annually the last weekend in July with the Texas International Apple Festival.

The wonder of apples is celebrated every day at the **Love Creek Orchards Cider Mill and Country Store.** At this store on Main Street in Medina, you will find apple cider, apple syrup, apple butters, apple jellies, apple cookies, apple pie, apple strudel, apple ice cream, and several varieties of unadulterated apples. One of those spiffy apple peelers is mounted on the counter, so the kids can peel their fresh

Granny Smith, McIntosh, or Red Delicious. Local arts and crafts, many with an apple motif, are also for sale. You can even buy saplings with an apple motif. Their address is Main Street Medina, Highway 16; call (210) 589-2588. Open Monday through Saturday, 9 A.M. to 5 P.M., and Sunday, 1 to 5 P.M.

Las Campanas Guest Ranch. You half expect to hear Twilight Zone's "duh-duh-duh-duh" as you pass through the front gate of Las Campanas. One moment you are in Vanderpool, Texas, and the next you are on Africa's Serengeti Plain. Over twenty varieties of exotic game as well as native game roam 2,500 acres of sparingly cross-fenced Hill Country. Oryx, elk, eland, kudu, wildebeest, black buck, and mouflon sheep have found safe harbor with owner Ernst Schneider. Only the native white-tailed does are harvested to stabilize the doe-buck ratio. The exotics are not hunted. As a result, the animals are merely watchful as the tour jeep rumbles past. Ernst jokes that he has coached them to pose for pictures.

Las Campanas can accommodate up to sixteen guests per night and in addition to photo safaris, offers catch and release fishing, hiking, bird watching, swimming, and tennis. And then there is the food. The Las Campanas brochure says "feast on exquisite gourmet cuisine." That is a tasteful understatement. Las Campanas is open for overnight guests from April to mid-December. (During the Texas winter, the owner goes to his native Namibia for the African summer.) For reservations and rate information, call (210) 966-3431, FAX (210) 966-6131, or write P.O. Box 238, Vanderpool, Texas 78885. $$$$

If *Texas Highways* magazine were to conduct one of their Readers' Choice surveys to select the state's prettiest stretches of road, one of my suggestions would be **Ranch Road 337** between Medina and Vanderpool, which is on the way to Lost Maples State Natural Area. Maps drawn before 1980 will not show this piece of asphalt, since it was not completed until that year. Yellow-square-on-tiptoe signs warn about Falling Rock, Earth Slides, and Hill (should read Big Hill). At least one of the three is guaranteed.

Highway 337 courses east-west through Hill Country surrounded by eroding fingers of the Edwards Plateau. It climbs the finger web and burrows through knuckles of gray Edwards limestone, yellow-tan Glen Rose limestone, and shale. These burrows, better known as roadcuts, provide glimpses of geological history.

Darwin Spearing explains the area's geology in his outstanding book, *Roadside Geology of Texas:*

> All the rocks in this area are early Cretaceous in age, deposited over
> millions of years in warm, shallow seas that once covered Texas.
> The Glen Rose formation, a collection of limestone, shale, marl,
> and siltstone beds, was deposited along the shifting margins of the
> sea where dinosaurs roamed in great numbers, leaving their foot-
> prints in the sands. The Cretaceous sea then spread over Texas in
> earnest, depositing thick layers of solid marine limestone, called the
> Edwards limestone, over the Glen Rose beds. This sequence of
> strata, Glen Rose below, and Edward above, is found throughout
> the area.

Even if you don't find hills that have been sliced open for our perusal (and for building the road) all that interesting, the surrounding in-tact hills are captivating. Fellow Texans, look around and be proud. In its full glory, this is your Hill Country.

Wimberley
Back to the Fifties at Blue Hole

This place you say you're looking for
It's a place I used to know
Don't know the number of the road
But I can tell you how to go
Head on down till the pavement ends
Used to go back there now and then
I used to know it like the back of my hand
When I was just a boy.
—James McMurtry, "Vague Directions"

There are a lot of places that I would rather go than a theme park. This whole book is about places that I would rather go than a theme park. Water parks are the most objectionable. They are hot, dirty, smelly, crowded, unsightly, and scary. These, my haughty opinions, are apparently unshared by the thousands of visitors that converge on theme parks every day and pay a lot of money to negotiate water troughs.

If you are crazy about water parks, you may not be interested in a place like Blue Hole that is cool, quiet, and pretty. That is okay. I do not take it personally. Have a nice day at the water park.

Blue Hole is an old-fashioned swimming hole on Cypress Creek, a spring-fed tributary of the Blanco River on the outskirts of Wimberley (population 2,447). The creek varies from ankle-cooling deep to thirteen feet. The deeper areas are at the base of two huge bald cypress trees that are fitted out with metal rings suspended by chains, just right for swinging away from shore and plopping in the clear, sixty-five-degree water.

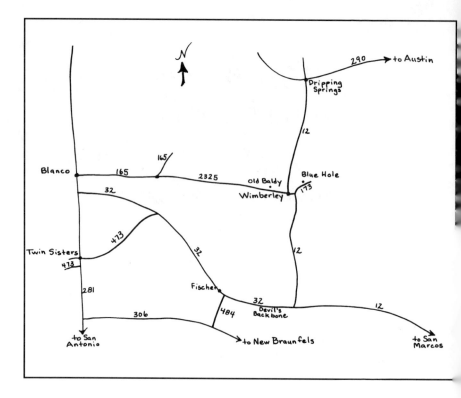

On the grassy banks are about twenty wooden picnic tables, flush toilets, and a water faucet. And, folks, that is about all there is to Blue Hole—that and the backdrop of a limestone escarpment and the shushing bald cypress trees with their shade umbrella.

Blue Hole is defined as much by what it lacks as by what it offers. There are no shrieking lifeguards or people waiting in long lines for a god-awful scary zip through a plastic conduit. There is no scorching concrete. Absent is the waft of that suntan oil that reeks of coconuts. Shade obviates that olfactory obtrusion.

Far away are the muddling crowds and the video game parlors and, come to think of it, just about every other reminder that I am not a little girl in the 1950s. Blue Hole offers old-fashioned fun and is a splendid spot for checking your eyelids for holes while you are lying back in a brought-along lawn chair. If you know what to look for, you can spot an occasional volunteer watermelon vine under a picnic table.

Blue Hole Recreation Club, as it is now called, has been open to the public since 1928. Insurance and tax legislation constraints put

Blue Hole, Wimberley

the term "recreation club" in Blue Hole. What this means to the day vacation crowd is that you pay a daily unlimited membership fee plus a per person walk-in fee. Children under three are free. For a family of four this adds up to less than half what a single ticket at the water park will set you back. For overnight guests, there are rustic and hook-up campsite facilities, also very reasonably priced.

If you find Blue Hole as peaceful and satisfying as I do, you may want to consider a seasonal membership. In a fancy restaurant, you may then be overheard to say (in an appropriately snitty tone), "We have unlimited membership privileges at Blue Hole Recreation Club." Those seated nearby will have no idea how much better that is than a membership at, say, Sonterra Country Club.

Day use of Blue Hole is from 9 A.M. to 8 P.M. The swimming hole is open from April through October. Blue Hole is located about .4 mile east of Wimberley off County Road 173. Entering Wimberley by way of State Road 12, go to the square (which is really more of a triangle) and turn right (east) on 173. Turn left after you pass the cemetery. The registration house is on the left near where the pavement ends. The telephone number is (512) 847-9127.

IN THE AREA AND ALONG THE WAY

It is a bit difficult to find the bottom of the steps leading to **Mount Alberta (Old Baldy)** and a bit strenuous to climb the 218 steps to the top, but worth the heartbeats if you have a healthy imagination. At the top of Mount Alberta, also called Old Baldy because of the sparsity of trees, is a rock dance floor. A few pieces are missing here and there, and the view from the summit includes more rooftops and radio towers than forty years ago when it was first built, but your imagination can edit those intrusions.

In 1950 Ed James of Eagle Rock Resort (now called Woodcreek Resort) commissioned construction of the steps and dance floor on this, the highest hill. For a short time there was even a jukebox up there. Imagine some enchanted evening, with the stars above, in the arms of your first love, shuffling to the music of a jukebox. You really would be on top of the world.

Mount Alberta is reached by heading northwest from Wimberley on State Road 2325 (off of State Road 12). Turn right into Woodcreek

Steps to the top of Old Baldy, Wimberley

Resort onto Woodcreek Drive. Take the first right which is El Camino Real, go a couple of blocks to a T in the road and turn right onto La Toya, which curves around and eventually encircles the base of Mount Alberta. The steps are on the left of the road if you are circling the base counterclockwise, with a parking space on the right side of the road. The climb is free.

Woolsey's Ice Cream Parlor and Deli is located on the square (I still say it is a triangle) in Wimberley. This family-oriented restaurant has deli-style sandwiches and Blue Bell ice cream. Sliced turkey sandwich and soup-of-the-day are on the menu. Open every day from 11:30 A.M. to 5:30 P.M. Call (512) 847-3333. $$

I would be remiss if I neglected to mention that Wimberley is an **artist colony** of sorts. Perhaps that is why the square is shaped like a triangle—the square has an artistic design. Numerous shops offer paintings, sculpture, jewelry, wall hangings, pottery, wreaths, wind chimes, and crafts. (You will, however, have to go to Fredericksburg if you want to find a mounted chicken in a basket.) The first Saturday of each month is Wimberley Market Days.

Devil's Backbone is a stretch of highway along a ridge in the Balcones Fault Zone with panoramic views of the Texas Hill Country. About ten million years ago, the earth slowly hiccuped and cracked, forming the Balcones Fault Zone. A fault zone is a great place to live—extruded rocks to build stuff with, natural springs, hills with trees on one side and prairies for farming on the other side. Devil's Backbone is smoothed and paved and a part of State Road 32 about 5 miles west of the junction with State Road 12 to Wimberley.

If Blue Hole takes you back to the 1950s, **Fischer Store and Post Office** in Fischer (population 20) will take you back even further. Located 13 miles southeast of Blanco on State Road 32, this barn-sized corrugated tin structure has served as a post office and store since 1902, when it was built by Hermann Fischer. A member of the Fischer family has been postmaster or postmistress ever since. The current Fischer tending the window is Gertrude Fischer, a sixtyish woman who tries to be grouchy. Grouchiness and the layers of old dust that cover the empty display cases will not stave off the ultimate demise of this anachronism. It is only a matter of time before an enterprising young couple wrests it from the 1930s and transforms it into a bed-and-breakfast or a lofted restaurant with exquisite fodder and a handsome wine list. For now, you can stop for a soda and a bag of chips. There are no bathrooms, just an outhouse with a slatted view of the highway.

Yoakum
History Trails to Cowhide Sales

Lose the track of time, and let it flow back.
Stoke the ancient furnace into flames.
Running barefoot in the cinders of the Mo-Pac.
Hopping bedtime rides with the outlaw Jesse James.
—Kinky Friedman, "Silver Eagle Express"

Yoakum (population 5,960) claims to be the Leather Capital of the World and with good cause—there are eleven leather factories in Yoakum. If Dad needs boots or Mom needs a purse or the kids need belts, go to Yoakum. Texas leather goods make unique gifts, too. That spinster aunt in Ohio might be delighted to receive some fringed chaps or some spurs and a whip. You never can tell.

Yoakum's history is anything but Rexall cowboy caliber. The land on which it stands was a Chisholm Trail gathering spot for some of the estimated ten million Longhorn cattle destined for Abilene, Kansas, and points north between 1867 and 1900. The glory days of cattle drives were stemmed by barbed wire and the railroad, but Yoakum sprang from the latter, becoming a central loading site for the San Antonio and Aransas Pass (SAP) line.

The town that developed was named for B. F. Yoakum, the line's traffic manager. Carloads of cattle headed for San Antonio, Houston, Corpus Christi, and Waco originated in Yoakum. Yoakum also served as the line's shop site where engines and luxury passenger cars were assembled and repaired. A roundhouse, where the huge locomotives were rotated, was also in Yoakum. Business was booming—Yoakum had six hotels, five live-stage theaters, and two opera houses.

The railroad meant packing houses, and packing houses meant hides. In 1919 Philip Welhausen opened Texas Hide and Leather

Company which is now called Tex Tan. Today, eleven leather companies operate in Yoakum, six on an international scale, justifying the Leather Capital nickname.

The factories used to take turns hosting guided tours. Insurance costs brought these up short. Factory tours are still conducted during the annual Land of Leather Days which is held the last weekend in February. The Chamber of Commerce has this information, so call (512) 293-2309.

You can't buy leather goods at the factories; however, the **Leather Capital Store,** at 123 West Grand, has a large assortment of leather products. Owners Leo and Barbara Smith can custom order leather goods and arrange for personalizing. The Leather Capital Store is a three-way cross among a factory store, a museum, and a tourist information center. A pronghorn, a longhorn steer, a hawk, and deer watch shoppers as they peruse the leather products, including saddles, halters and bridles, and the non-leather items, including ceramics, jewelry, Indian artifacts, wood carvings, and Western wear. The purses from the Circle Y Leather Factory are my favorites—I give one to my mom nearly every year for her birthday. The Leather Capital Store is open Monday through Saturday, 10 A.M. to 6:30 P.M. Their telephone number is (512) 293-7274.

An official museum, the **Yoakum Heritage Museum,** housed in the donated Elkins-Browning home, outlines the history of the Yoakum leather industry as well as the history of the cattle drives, the SAP Railroad, and the withered, but not forgotten, tomato industry.

Between the mid-1920s and mid-1930s, up to six hundred train carloads of tomatoes were shipped from Yoakum each growing season. Area farmers brought almost-ripe tomatoes to Yoakum where they were hand-sorted and then carefully packed in padded crates. A few of the rusting tomato sheds linger, a reminder of the days when Yoakum competed with Florida and Southern California for top honors in the tomato business.

Two walls of the museum are covered by registered cattle brands. The brands are numbered and a key explains each brand's meaning, issue date, and past and current users. Demystifying cattle brands is challenging. Take the letter *C* surrounded by a circle, for instance. My

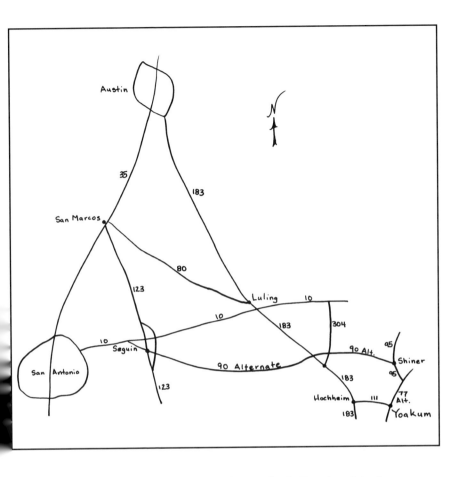

first guess would be that it stands for Circle C. But, it might just as well mean Lassoed Lazy U, O'Connor, Copyright, Ring around the Carbon, Zero C, or Tipsy Happy Face With Eyes Missing. The possibilities are endless, like a circle. How about Endless Circle C or C without End? If I ever knew, I have forgotten what it does stand for.

Between December 1 and December 31, except Christmas Day, the museum hosts the Annual Christmas Tree Forest. About seventy-five Christmas trees are decorated by local businesses, schools, civic organizations, and citizens. According to Dennis Rowan, executive director of the Yoakum Heritage Museum, approximately one-third of the museum's fifteen thousand yearly visitors come to see the Christmas trees. And, if they are like me, those visitors return to Yoakum the following Christmas season. KSAT-12 from San Antonio, *The*

Eyes of Texas television show, and *Texas Highways* magazine have all featured the Yoakum Annual Christmas Tree Forest. Warning: when you return home, your own Christmas tree will look anemic.

The Yoakum Heritage Museum is across the street from the elementary school at 312 Simpson and is open Monday through Saturday, 1 P.M. to 5 P.M., and on Sunday from 3 P.M. to 5 P.M. Schools can arrange morning tours by calling (512) 293-7022. Self-guided tours during the afternoon are one dollar for adults and free for kids.

All this talk about cattle and leather may leave you in the mood for some red meat. **Wieting's Steakhouse** is located near the edge of town at the junction of State Highways 77 Alternate and 111 West which is the road to Hochheim. The cafeteria line is open Tuesday through Saturday, 11 A.M. to 2 P.M., and serves two choices of beef, several steamed vegetables, cornbread, and salad. You can also have the vegetables and visit the salad bar. The supper hours are Tuesday through Thursday, 5 P.M. to 10 P.M., and Friday and Saturday, 5 P.M. to 11 P.M. Sunday hours are from 11 A.M. to 9 P.M. The restaurant is closed on Monday. Call (512) 293-7502. The Rotary Club, Ladies' Pilot Club, Garden Club, and Kiwanis Club meet here, if that gives you a feel for this family-oriented, community-centered restaurant. $$

State Highway 111 is an alternate way home through Hochheim. This route adds little travel time and is a nice roll through blackland prairies and post oak savannah, roughly paralleling the Guadalupe River. Wildflowers abound in spring.

ALONG THE WAY

Seguin (population 19,452) is named for the Tejano political leader Juan Nepomucena Seguín. A hero of the Texas Revolution, he fought in all the major battles, except the Alamo. Seguín was at the Alamo when the siege began, but Travis sent him and Antonio Cruz Arocha for reinforcements and Seguín missed the battle. Seguín was branded a traitor by the ruling Mexican government when he, Lorenza de Zavala, and José Navarro raised a company of volunteers from the San Antonio area. Among his military accomplishments were participating in the battles of Concepción and Bexar and providing rear guard for the settlers during the Runaway Scrape. After commanding

*Annual Christmas Tree Forest, Yoakum
Heritage Museum*

a regiment in the decisive Battle at San Jacinto, he was promoted to lieutenant colonel in the Texas Cavalry. From 1837 to 1840 Seguín served as senator from the Bexar District, and from 1841 to 1848 he served as mayor of San Antonio.

Despite his impressive record, Seguín was eventually the subject of malicious prejudice, as were many other "unnatural Mexicans," as Tejanos fighting on the side for independence had been called by Santa Anna. After Texas gained independence, a Spanish surname equated with loyalty to the despised Mexican government south of the Rio Grande in the minds of many Anglos. This left Tejanos without a home, denied rights in the Republic that they, too, had fought to establish.

Perhaps Seguín and other Tejanos could have avoided this catch-22 if they had died defending the Alamo, along with Juan Abamillo, Juan Antonio Badillo, Carlos Espalier, José Gregorio Esparza, Antonio Fuentes, Toribio Losoya, Andrés Nava, and Damacio Ximines.

Seguin has a beautiful public park on the Guadalupe River called **Max Starcke Park** and a five-foot pecan in front of the Guadalupe County courthouse on Austin Street. The pecan is made of concrete and metal but looks real, even up close. I want it on record that I don't think that the town's pride in its big pecan is silly, as a character

World's largest pecan, courthouse lawn, Seguin

in Sandra Cisneros' book *Woman Hollering Creek and Other Stories* thinks it is.

Gonzales (population 6,533) is discussed in the section about Ottine and Palmetto State Park. I won't say anything more about the grass needing to be watered.

Shiner (population 2,008) means the K. Spoetzl Brewery to most Texans. And, indeed, Texas' Own Little Brewery at 603 Brewery Street, off State Highway 95 North, deserves a side trip. The museum and gift shop are open daily from 9 A.M. to 1 P.M. and from 2 P.M. to 5 P.M., and on Saturday from 11 A.M. to 3 P.M. Brewery tours are at 11 A.M., Monday through Friday. Call them at (512) 594-3852.

The brewery tour is fun. The tour begins with a short history of the K. Spoetzl Brewery, beginning with the grassroot, or more accurately, barleyroot efforts of the local German and Czech farmers in 1909. The cheerful guide then leads the group through the brewery and explains the progression from sacks of feed to kegs of beer. The tour concludes at the bar or, as they call it, the Hospitality Room. No, thanks, I was driving, but it looked good. The tours are free.

I was lucky enough to be in Shiner on a clear, breezy February day which followed several days of South Texas drizzle. Every clothesline in Shiner was T-bar to T-bar full of flapping, clean clothes. Well-appointed clotheslines make me feel like all is right in the world. I associate them with the fragrance of my mother's line-dried, fresh-ironed pillowcases. Brewery to some. Clotheslines to me. Shiner is a special little town.

Hochheim (pronounced "hoe-hime" and rhymes with "no crime") is a shadow of its former self. It has a beautiful cemetery that dates to early immigrant days, with a historical marker telling a little about it. The Hochheim Cemetery is still being used. By that I mean, people are still buried there. What I mean to say is that the newly deceased are still being buried there. The population of Hochheim is 70, if you don't count the ones in the cemetery.

San Antonio
Doing the Tourist Thing

✸

I heard the thunder over Canaan
And I heard the angels cry
And their voices came revealing
As you live, so will you die.
—Roy Orbison, "Coming Home"

According to the Texas Department of Commerce, San Antonio's tourism and convention industry contributed over 1.5 billion dollars to the local economy in 1991. About ten million people visit the Alamo City every year, and with the aggressive promotion by the San Antonio Convention and Visitors Bureau, that number promises to swell.

There are shelves of books about San Antonio's tourist attractions. The *San Antonio Express-News* has a special weekend section in the Friday paper that lists current happenings in the area. *San Antonio Our Kids* is a free monthly publication that has a calendar with "things to do, places to go, people to see," as well as feature articles, movie and book reviews, and a professional directory of doctors, therapists, psychological testing, and so forth. You can pick up a copy at the take-one racks at H.E.B. grocery stores. Geared more towards adults is another free monthly publication called *Key: The Traveler's Magazine.* It is a purse-sized publication that has "sights, entertainment, events, shopping, dining, maps." It is available in most hotel lobbies.

The source list goes on. But, this is *my* book, so I get to tell about *my* favorite stuff.

I work with a man who grew up in Maine. There is such a thing as Maine humor, but I am not entirely sure he was kidding when he said, "I don't understand why the Texans chose to defend the

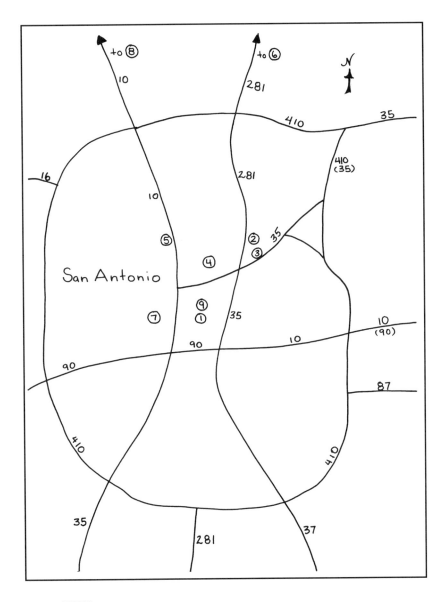

KEY:
1. Alamo
2. Botanical Garden
3. Quadrangle
4. Planetarium
5. Cool Crest
6. Guadalupe River State Park
7. Karam's
8. Friedrich Park
9. Vietnam Veterans Memorial

Alamo. The Marriott would have given them a better vantage point."

First-time visitors to the Alamo are often surprised at its downtown location at the bottom of a canyon of tall buildings. With the post office to the north, the Menger Hotel to the east, Rivercenter Mall to the south, and the *raspa* vendors to the west, one might expect the Alamo to be swallowed in the city's bustle. Those dreading another tawdry tourist trap are in for a sobering surprise. The Alamo is a chapel. Men are asked to remove their hats, and everyone is asked to speak in their church and synagogue voices.

There is a gnomic utterance that I must paraphrase because I can't remember, but it goes something like, "You like someone because of what they are. You love someone in spite of what they are." So it is with me and the Alamo. Beneath the misty-eyed story about men fighting for liberty lie other reasons for Americans going to northern Mexico looking for a rumble. They wanted land, they wanted money, and they wanted power. In spite of these detracting details, I still love the Alamo. It is a Texas icon.

No Texan should live a full measure without attending a memorial service for the heroes of the Alamo. This simple and dignified ceremony is held every year in the Alamo Chapel on March 6, the day the Alamo fell. It begins at 2:30 in the afternoon. Seating is limited, and members of the Daughters of the Republic of Texas are given priority. A labyrinth of coincidences allowed me to attend the Alamo memorial service in 1992. I count it as one of the most significant experiences of my life.

The service began with presentation of the colors by soldiers from Lackland Air Force Base, all standing as the color guard and flags passed to the front of the chapel. The invocation was offered by Sister Elizabeth Anne Sueltenfuss, president of Our Lady of the Lake University. Henry Holloway, director of music at Laurel Heights United Methodist Church (and my labyrinth-solver), sang "Amazing Grace." Singing a cappella, the familiar strains resounding from the chapel roof, Mr. Holloway made prayer for us. Hands stayed folded.

Mrs. Bruce Nell Gooler of the Daughters of the Republic of Texas read the ninetieth psalm: "Lord, thou hast been our dwelling place in all generations. Before the mountains were brought forth, or ever thou hadst formed the earth and the world, even from everlasting to everlasting, thou are God."

As David Foster, chaplain of the Alamo Mission Chapter of the Daughters of the Republic of Texas read "Call Out Their Names Again," five candles were lit, one each for William B. Travis, James B. Bonham, James Bowie, and David Crockett, and the last for the other 184 Alamo defenders. He recited:

> *Call out the names of these Texans again,*
> *Come and view the place where they last stood,*
> *Travis and Crockett, Bowie, Bonham—men*
> *Who bought this plot of earth with their own blood.*
>
> *Call out the name of Bowie on the cot*
> *Who knew that death was near but chose to stay;*
> *Call out the name of every patriot*
> *Who dared cross the line that day.*
>
> *These men are gone. Their wars are done. The mold*
> *Has claimed their bones. Speak now with softened breath*
> *Their names.*
>
> *Call out their names again—these bold*
> *Texans who were so unafraid of death.*
> —Marvin Davis Winsett, "Call Out Their Names Again"

The defenders of the Alamo were born in twenty-one states of the United States and seven countries, including Mexico, the nation where the battle occurred. In alphabetical order, each state flag and then each national flag of the birthplaces of the Alamo defenders was presented, slowly dipped, and snapped to attention. Mexico's flag of 1824 was presented after the last state (Virginia) and before the first nation (Denmark), as if the Tejanos (Mexicans born in Texas) did not fit into either category. In a very real sense this is true. Those nine Alamo defenders were of a singular type—they were the only men defending native soil.

Liz Carpenter, journalist and author, gave the address, which was about courage and sacrifice. Mr. Holloway sang "Faith of Our Fathers," which was about truth and love. Sister Elizabeth offered the benediction, which was about hope and forgiveness. The ceremony concluded with echo taps. A bugler near the front of the chapel sounded the familiar four notes, with a soft echo from a second bugler at the back of the chapel. By the final, muted strains, there were few dry eyes.

The Daughters of the Republic of Texas care for and guard the Alamo and put on the memorial service each year. That is why they have first dibs on seats at the service.

I was only thinly aware of the Daughters of the Republic of Texas until a clerk at the Alamo Museum gift shop (a great place to buy books, by the way) asked me, "Are you a Daughter?" (It seems that members of the Daughters of the Republic of Texas enjoy a 10 percent discount on purchases from the gift shop.) It took me a moment to catch on that she meant Daughter, as in Daughter of the Republic of Texas, rather than a female offspring. I answered, "No. But, how do I go about becoming a Daughter?"

Knowing that I was ineligible if I had to ask, she informed me that one must be able to prove that one is a direct descendant from someone who lived in Texas during the years that it was a Republic (between 1836 and 1845). I said, "Oh, I see," but I thought, "Well, do tell."

That leaves me out. I am only a third generation Texan. This is unfortunate for me, but it is even more unfortunate for the Daughters. Their membership requirement excludes some of us that would venerate such an affiliation. Like naturalized Americans with perspective, we relatively recent Texas arrivals may cherish our state even more than those who were born with a Lone Star flag in their fists.

I have a plan that would benefit all concerned with reverence for and preservation of Texas history—create a subchapter and call it the Stepdaughters of the Republic of Texas. Genealogy requirements would be waived, but applicants must pass a comprehensive Texas history test and be able to recite the Alamo muster roll and the Texas Declaration of Independence (or the plain old Declaration of Independence—they are virtually the same.) The Stepdaughters would be assigned the dreary tasks, but membership would still have its privileges. Stepdaughters could have the 10 percent discount in the gift shop and, like the Real Daughters, they would be allowed to mingle with the throng visiting the Alamo and shout, "Shhh!"

The Alamo is open Monday through Saturday from 9 A.M. to 5:30 P.M. and on Sunday from 10 A.M. to 5:30 P.M. It is closed on December 24 and 25. There is no admission fee, but there is a donation box. I think a check made out for $1.89 or $18.90 would be appropriate.

AFTER THE ALAMO

The **Riverwalk,** the **Alamo,** and **El Mercado** (the Mexican market) head the list of why San Antonio, along with New Orleans, New York City, and San Francisco, is one of America's most unique cities. That may be so. I agree with the part about the Alamo—it is one of my three favorite things about San Antonio. (The other two are my job and signs pointing to Austin.)

Instead of going to New Orleans for Mardi Gras, we go to South Louisiana—Mamou, Henderson, Breaux Bridge, and Saint Martinville. These little towns are in the strong-beating heart of Acadiana—Cajun country. (Bear with me, I haven't forgotten that I am talking about the San Antonio Riverwalk.) It was from a sixty-year old Cajun at La Grande Boucherie Des Cajuns in Saint Martinville that I got the rundown on the San Antonio Riverwalk. He was telling me what he liked best about his recent visit: "Dat Alamoa reyal, reyal goowood, but ah spen' dah mos' time dere in dah middle of dah town on dah bayou." The San Antonio Bayouwalk does have a certain panache, but I doubt if the new name will catch on.

I regret being a killjoy, but the Riverwalk and El Mercado don't do all that much for me; however, there are other places in San Antonio that I can suggest to take children. By now, you have probably gathered that theme parks will not be on slate.

San Antonio Botanical Garden is located at 555 Funston off North New Braunfels. It is open from 9 A.M. to 6 P.M., Tuesday through Sunday. Opened in 1980 and getting better with age, the Botanical Garden is situated on thirty-three acres adjacent to Fort Sam Houston. Featured gardens include the Japanese Garden, the Rose Garden, the Old Fashioned Garden, the Herb Garden, the Garden for the Blind, the Sacred Garden, and the Xeriscape Garden. The less manicured areas of Botanical Garden fade from trees and vegetation common in the Hill Country to those of the East Texas pineywoods. The eastern edge of the park is a patch of South Texas plains with sotol and century plants.

The geodesic, glass-paneled conservatory complex was completed in 1988. These glass sheds maintain specific humidities and temperatures for desert plants, tropical plants, ferns, and palms. Outlets periodically mist out clouds. It's real neat.

My favorite place at Botanical, as my family has come to call it over the years, is a metal park bench overlooking the grassy outdoor amphitheater. In a previous life, its limestone walls were part of a spring water reservoir that supplied San Antonio's water needs. The limestone walls and the clean slope of grass are restful, but it is the line of sycamore trees that makes me be still and listen. The sound of wind in sycamore leaves is a whisper of solace.

Admission for adults is a few dollars. For exact prices call (210) 821-5115.

The **Quadrangle** is located on the southwest edge of Fort Sam Houston and is the headquarters of the Fifth U.S. Army. The Quadrangle was first occupied in December, 1879, and is the oldest building at Fort Sam, the abbreviated name of Fort Sam Houston. The Quadrangle was built like a frontier fort with thick, high walls on the outside and doors opening into the two-block square courtyard. The courtyard is now safe harbor for deer, ducks, chickens, rabbits, and peacocks. Accustomed to children, these creatures are quite tame and many let you pet them. During one visit, one of the does became enthralled with my son, at the time four years old, and stalked him, licking his cheeks and hair until he was chapped and hair-plastered. My younger sister took a snapshot because I was laughing too hard to hold the camera still.

In the center of the courtyard stands the eight-story clock tower. In volume three of *Off the Beaten Trail,* Ed Syers tells the rich history of Fort Sam Houston through the old clock face's "indelible memory." He names the great men who had heard the bell's toll—Teddy Roosevelt, John J. Pershing, Dwight Eisenhower, and many others. He describes the view from the tower—the San Antonio

River to the south, disarmed rockets to the southwest, barracks to the north: "What else from that clock tower? Some of the others you can see from the tower . . . under the crosses beyond the hill northeast; many, many more beneath them, far away. That's the view from Fort Sam's watchtower, when the bell rings clear. For whom, the bell? You. Me. Our kids. Our land. Old Army's proudest best."

The Quadrangle is open every day from 5:45 A.M. until 9 P.M. during daylight savings months (April to October) and from 5:45 A.M. until 7 P.M. the rest of the year. Please remember to take some carrots for the deer and rabbits, and some corn for the ducks (a sign says "no bread").

For more information about the hours that the Quadrangle is open, call (210) 221-0522. Turn east off Broadway on Grayson, go six blocks, passing parade grounds partially surrounded by enormous homes. At the end of the parade grounds is the Quadrangle, its entrance decorated with a young, saluting soldier. The Quadrangle can also be reached by exiting North New Braunfels off Interstate Highway 35 South, then four blocks to Grayson. There is no admission charge.

The **San Antonio College Planetarium** is located near the middle of the college campus and is reached by turning east on Park off San Pedro Avenue. The silver dome of the planetarium is on the left in the second block. To hear a recorded message about the schedule of shows, call (210) 733-2910. In general, the planetarium is open when college is in session. During the fall and spring semesters, shows are at 5 P.M., 6:30 P.M., and 8 P.M. on Sunday evenings. There is no admission charge, but seating is limited to one hundred ceiling-gazers. Also, because of the content of the shows, the 5 P.M. show is restricted to children that are at least four years old. The 6:30 P.M. and 8 P.M. shows require that children be at least six years old.

I probably wouldn't enjoy **Cool Crest Miniature Golf Course** if it weren't for the terraced arrangement of the thirty-six-hole course, the breezy views of downtown San Antonio, the well-tended flowers and banana trees, and the Coke machine with paper cups and crushed ice. I don't generally enjoy playing miniature golf, but Cool Crest is different. Maybe that is why it has been in its same location with a

San Antonio college Planetarium

steady stream of grounds rules–following patrons since 1937—in over fifty years of operation, the police have never had to be called.

The golf course has its original owners, Mr. and Mrs. Harold Metzger. On the front of the scorecard is the following statement: "We have tried earnestly to provide you with an atmosphere of beauty, music, and fun." Go judge for yourself if the Metzgers have succeeded.

Cool Crest Miniature Golf Course is at 1402 Fredericksburg Road next to the Oak Farms Dairy. It is open every day, weather permitting, from 2 P.M. until midnight. Greens fees are very reasonable—the whole family can play eighteen holes for less than the cost of a theme park ticket. The phone number, until they got modern, was PE 2-0222. Now it is (210) 732-0222. (PE stood for Pershing.)

Karam's Mexican Dining Room is at 121 North Zarzamora Street at the intersection with West Commerce. The best Mexican food restaurant in San Antonio is a tough call. If a Mexican food restaurant is marginal, it does not survive *uno momento*. Even if it is pretty good, the others usually crowd it out. If longevity is any indication, Karam's is a keeper. Opened in 1946, this family-owned, family-operated, and family-oriented restaurant on the near west side of downtown is my top pick. Shiny tile floors below, scores of piñatas above, and pleasant staff serving great Mexican food in between make for a *muy bueno* meal. Dieters can order chicken fajita taco salad, hold the guacamole. Open Sunday through Thursday, 11 A.M. to 10 P.M., Friday and Saturday, 11 A.M. to 11 P.M. Call (210) 433-0111. $$$

Friedrich Wilderness Park is a San Antonio–owned public park 20 miles west of the Alamo off Interstate Highway 10 West. Exit at Boerne Stage Road/Leon Springs, turn left, then left again to the IH-10 East access road. A brown sign directs you right (south) on Oak. The park has a few picnic tables near the parking lot, rest rooms, a drinking fountain, and nearly 5 miles of trails looping through 232 acres of Hill Country.

The trails meander among native stands of old cedar trees, which are really ashe junipers (*Juniperus ashei*). Some of these trees are over two hundred years old. Shaggy old cedar trees creak and grind when the wind blows, begrudging the wind's prying. The medley of wind and creaking cedar trees is very restful. That will only make sense to those who have stopped to listen to it. In the spring the redbud trees grab center stage for about a month with a surge of pink blossoms.

The trails are well-marked and -markered—eighty-four numbered wooden markers are described in the park brochure, which is available at the trailhead. The brochure also includes a map and descriptions of the various nature trails. To hike all the trails takes about three hours. The brochure indicates that the Fern Del Trail, which is about one-fourth mile, takes forty-five minutes to hike. It took us about ten minutes and is one of the prettiest parts of the park.

The park is open from 8 A.M. to 5 P.M., Wednesday through Sunday. All visitors must leave by 5 P.M. The park is smoke-free and pet-free. Guided hikes are on the first Saturday of each month at 9 A.M. For information about these hikes and other organized activities at Friedrich Park, call (210) 698-1057, or write Friends of Friedrich Wilderness Park, P.O. Box 691371, San Antonio, Texas 78269-1371. There is no admission fee to the park, but if you are interested in becoming one of the Friends, you can write them at the address above.

Guadalupe River State Park and the contiguous **Honey Creek State Natural Area** are located 30 miles north of San Antonio on State Highway 46, 7 miles west of its intersection with U.S. Highway 281 and 13 miles east of its intersection with IH-10. Guadalupe River State Park is 1,900 acres of Hill Country crossed by its peridot-green, occasionally tumultuous, namesake. Day users can swim and wade, hike, fish, canoe, and picnic. Swimming in the Guadalupe River is irresistible on a hot July afternoon. There are no lifeguards, but the river is shallow in the park's main swimming area. Winter weekday visits should be preceded by a phone call to the park to make sure that a gun-siting exercise (otherwise known as a public hunt) is not underway. Day use requires the usual state park entrance fee, unless you have a Texas Conservation Passport, which gets you through the gate for free (see Appendix 1). For information about Guadalupe River State Park, call (210) 438-2656 between 8 A.M. and 5 P.M., or write Park Superintendent, Guadalupe River State Park, HC 54, Box 2087, Bulverde, Texas 78163.

With prior reservations, overnight visitors have their choice of 48 electrical campsites with water, 37 non-electrical campsites with water, or 20 non-electrical walk-in campsites with water. Rest rooms are at park headquarters and in the camping areas. Reservations for campsites can be made by calling (512) 389-8900 (see Appendix 1).

Holders of the Texas Conservation Passport can also participate in guided hikes through the Honey Creek State Natural Area on most Saturday mornings at nine. (Call the park before you leave home to make sure that a hike is planned.) These easy walks last around two and a half hours and cover about a mile of rocky ground with numerous pauses by the Texas Parks and Wildlife guide to explain the area's history, geology, plants, and animals. If the guide is Penny Solís,

"Hill 881 South," Vietnam memorial by Austin Deuel, San Antonio

park naturalist, discussion of vegetation is favored, since plants are Penny's prime interest.

The **Honey Creek State Natural Area** is a 1,825-acre tract which was once a working ranch. In 1980 the Texas Nature Conservancy purchased the land, and in 1985 the Honey Creek State Natural Area was transferred to the Texas Parks and Wildlife Department. Since 1980 efforts have been underway to restore the habitat to some semblance of what it was before the 1860s. It was then that German settlers tried to farm it and, failing at that, used it for pasture.

When pressed into service, the deceptively thin and fragile topsoil of the Hill Country fares poorly. The overlying humus, that organic, mulch-like layer of decayed and decaying plants, is destroyed, and the topsoil becomes easy prey for erosion. With little soil to nurture it, the native grasses wane. Woody plants, like the now ubiquitous ashe juniper (called cedar trees by ranchers, usually with a qualifying term), claim hills once covered by soil-clutching grass. Adding insult to invasion, the vilified burgeoning populations of white-tailed deer browse on tender sprouts of grass.

Through prescribed burns and seasonal sprout assistance measures, parts of the Honey Creek State Natural Area are becoming more natural. The difference between restored and preserved (in other words, left alone) areas is apparent, even to untrained eyes such as mine. The preserved areas are thick with ashe juniper and essentially devoid of grass. In contrast, the restored areas have fields of native grasses such as little bluestem, indiangrass, and switchgrass, which beckon birds and other wildlife. The restoration efforts are in earnest and are ongoing but are thwarted by lack of funds.

The guided walk goes to the banks of Honey Creek, a spring-fed tributary of the Guadalupe River. The spring originates on private property an undisclosed distance from the park boundaries. Bald cypress trees crowd the creek's banks which, during the warm months, are home to a knot of shy little frogs.

The hike begins and ends at the Rust Visitor Center which is a recycled German farmhouse. Inside are nature exhibits, including a display about paper wasps, gall wasps, and mud daubers. I have been more regardful of wasps since an organic gardener showed me a mud dauber nest full of dead black widow spiders and told me that yellow jackets eat web worms. Since then, I have left wasp nests alone unless they threaten an unavoidable path. So far, the wasps have done the same for me.

Vietnam Veterans Memorial is a bronze sculpture which shows a marine radioman kneeling beside a fallen comrade. His right hand is at the neck of his fellow soldier, as if searching for a pulse. Anguished, he looks skyward for the rescue helicopter or for divine intervention. The sculpture is by Austin Deuel, a marine combat artist, and is entitled *Hill 881 South*. The statue was dedicated on Veterans Day in 1986. It is located in Veterans Memorial Plaza on Auditorium Circle near Municipal Auditorium. The grass and flowers are well tended.

Austin
Going Home—McKinney Falls State Park

❂

*. . . but, my peace of mind
is a place I go when I close my eyes.*
—Nanci Griffith, "Hometown Streets"

McKinney Falls State Park is snuggled up against the southeast corner of Austin. If I were a state park, I would snuggle up to Austin, too.

I love Austin. I love the Capitol, the bike lanes, and Oat Willie's. I love the artificial moons, the want ads of the *Austin Chronicle,* and Scholz's. I love the peddlers on the Drag, the healing waters of Barton Springs, and the Austin Sound. Mercy, mercy, that Austin Sound. I love Northwest Park and Pease Park and Zilker Park and Eastwood Park. I love the memories of the Armadillo Decade, before Freda was Marcia and Jerry Jeff was sober. Most of all, I love Austin's stubborn refusal to sit up straight and act like a proper capital city.

If I seem a bit flushed and breathless, it is because I am in love with Austin—adolescent, fault-denying love. When I crest the hill at Onion Creek, the asphalt slab turns to yellow brick.

Others must be relied upon to give objective information. I cannot seem to get a grip on myself when I write about Austin. Blow a kiss from me when you are there.

Like many of his beautifully written and illustrated books for children, Chris Van Allsburg's book, *Just a Dream,* carries an important message. Walter, the main character, has a dream, a nightmare, really, about the consequences of environmental neglect. The nightmare is followed by a second dream about a nurtured and nurturing planet. Walter decides to enter the nurturing circle.

Austin has its own rendering of Walter's nightmare. Five-thousand-visitor-a-day-popular McKinney Falls State Park suffered an embar-

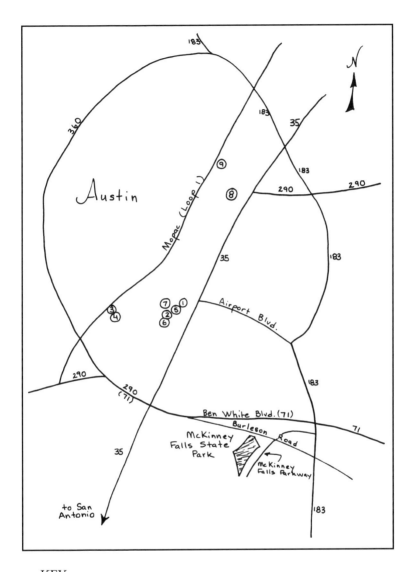

KEY:
1. Texas Memorial Museum
2. Congress Avenue Bridge
3. Austin Nature Center
   and Zilker Preserve
4. Zilker Park
5. Austin Visitor Center
6. Terra Toys
7. Capitol
8. Frisco's
9. Northwest Park

rassing suspension of swimming in 1981 after children from Saint Elmo School took sick after swimming there. Studies showed that the source of the tainted water was the upstream City of Austin Williamson Wastewater Treatment Plant. The plant was closed in 1985, but low-spirited spokespeople predicted that Onion Creek might never recover from the spoilage. The number of park visitors plummeted.

But my beloved Austin was underestimated. McKinney Falls State Park was reopened to swimmers in June of 1993. Efforts by volunteers, the Texas Parks and Wildlife Department, the Austin City Council, Travis County officials, the *Austin American-Statesman,* the Barton Springs/Edwards Aquifer Conservation District, the Texas Water Commission, and the passage of time have undone much of the damage. Onion Creek is still fragile and guidelines are in place for closure if water quality is marginal for swimming and wading; however, we can smile now. This is a victory. The good guys are winning. The kids can go swimming.

Although swimming and wading are permitted in Onion Creek and Williamson Creek anywhere in the park, there are two main swimming areas at McKinney Falls State Park. The namesake falls, **McKinney Falls** is near the junction of Onion Creek and Williamson Creek. The **Upper Falls** is upstream on Onion Creek. McKinney Falls (or Lower Falls, as it is sometimes called) is the more popular of the two swimming areas, but Upper Falls is a little easier to get to. Both swimming areas are rimmed by a semicircle of limestone, clawed into serpentine channels by Onion Creek. Depending on rainfall, the falls vary from big trickles to bona fide falls. Both swimming areas have caliche and sand beaches and plenty of shade.

The swimming areas are unimproved, which means that they are natural waterways, not a swimming pool or an improved waterway like Barton Springs. There are no lifeguards on duty, and adults are responsible for minor children.

The swimming areas are open from dawn to dark, May 1 through September 30. The water is tested at least three days per week. If the water is dirty or has too many bacteria, swimming advisories are posted at the park entrance. Advisories are also posted if there are severe weather or flood conditions. You can learn of swimming conditions by calling the twenty-four-hour park hotline at (512) 243-0848.

McKinney Falls State Park also has 3 miles of paved hike and bike trails—the longest in the state park system—and a three-fourth–mile interpretive nature trail called the **Rock Shelter Trail**. This trail is easy and takes less than an hour to hike, even if you pause to read the guidebook at all sixteen of the numbered markers. The Rock Shelter Trail originates near the Smith Visitor Center and follows along Onion Creek. It ducks beneath limestone shelves which were once home to ancient Amerinds. Now the limestone bellies are meeting spots for quaking, tangled tribes of harmless daddy longlegs.

The marked trail loops back towards the Visitor Center before reaching McKinney Falls; however, if you venture off the beaten trail at marker 7 and continue to follow Onion Creek for .25 miles you will reach the limestone rim overlooking McKinney Falls. The water in Onion Creek that forms the falls has many sources: the Edwards Aquifer, spring water, rainwater runoff, and water from seven tributary creeks, the largest of which is Williamson Creek. More amazing than the water's sundry sources is the limestone bed over which the creek runs. It is full of shallow eddy pits—places where the water has gotten a toehold and swirled a depression in the rock. I find these water-whittled patterns enormously intriguing.

The **Smith Visitor Center** overlooks the Upper Falls and is geared towards children and adults who enjoy hands-on exhibits. The Touch Table has fossils, shells, bones, wasp nests (empty), seeds, turtle shells (also empty), antlers, and spiders frozen in plastic resin. I accidentally dropped and cracked one of the resin domes holding a spider. Unspeakably sorry, I reported my bungle to Ms. Sapp, the park volunteer on duty. Her response: "Oh, don't worry. Accidents happen. We would rather have an occasional mishap than forbid visitors to touch our exhibit items. That's what they're there for."

The Smith Visitor Center is staffed by Texas State Park volunteers and is open on Saturday from 9 A.M. to 1 P.M. and on Sunday from 9 A.M. to 4 P.M. Guided hikes are year round on Saturdays and Sundays at 9:30 A.M., weather permitting. Special hikes include seasonal bird walks to see painted buntings. The customary day-use state park entrance fees apply. For more information about McKinney Falls State

McKinney Falls State Park

Park, call (512) 243-1643 between 8 A.M. and 5 P.M., or write Park Superintendent, McKinney Falls State Park, 7102 Scenic Loop, Austin, Texas 78744.

For the overnight crowd, there are eighty-four sought-after campsites, some with water only, some with water and electricity, and some with water, electricity, satellite discs, and fax machines (just kidding). For reservations call (512) 389-8900 (see Appendix 1).

To reach the park, exit Interstate Highway 35 at Ben White Boulevard. Go east .75 miles to Burleson Road. Turn right on Burleson Road and continue 2.75 miles to McKinney Falls Parkway. Turn right and go 1 mile to the park entrance.

ALSO IN AUSTIN

Texas Memorial Museum has that musty, muted atmosphere that only old museums, old churches, and old libraries can garner. It is not stuffy. Quite the contrary. The high ceilings, polished floors and filtered light just say, "Shhh. Let us now learn."

Instead of telling children that this museum specializes in geology, paleontology, natural history, and anthropology, tell them instead that they will see semiprecious and precious stones, dinosaur bones, a giant armadillo shell, a fish skeleton as big as a fishing boat, a sixteen-foot lady with big nostrils, stuffed snakes and lizards, and a wall of Huaxtec clay figurines. The latter are mother goddesses symbolizing growth and fertility. The word "fertility" always gets the attention of twelve-year olds.

During my college days at the University of Texas, roughly twenty years ago, the Texas Memorial Museum had a shrunken head and an exhibit detailing the process of shrinking heads. Last time I was there, I couldn't find it, which was disappointing. Perhaps it became politically incorrect or someone thought it was gauche.

Texas Memorial Museum is at 2400 Trinity on the east side of the University of Texas campus, two blocks north of Memorial Stadium, and three blocks west of the LBJ Library, where there is free parking. It is behind the A. Phimister Proctor—what a splendid name—bronze sculpture of *The Mustangs* on San Jacinto Street. It is open Monday through Friday from 9 A.M. to 5 P.M., on Saturday from 10 A.M. to 5 P.M., and on Sunday from 1 P.M. to 5 P.M. The museum is closed on major holidays. There is no admission fee, but you can leave a contribution if you like. If you must spend money, go to the museum gift shop. Call (512) 471-1605.

It is no coincidence that **Bat Conservation International** is based in Austin, since the Congress Avenue Bridge in Austin is the largest urban bat colony in North America. Like the previously discussed bats that roost near Comfort, the Congress Avenue bats leave their roost en masse around dusk on spring and summer nights. July and August are the best months for watching them leave for dinner, squeaking and reeking (slightly) of ammonia. It is rather a happening on summer nights, what with the bats soaring, the Austinites watching, and the streetlights blinking on.

"Bats" is one of the Discovery Box topics at the **Austin Nature Center.** Discovery Boxes are hands-on teaching materials for children that can be checked out by an adult at the Visitor Pavilion. Information stations (tables at a child's height level with stuff to look at and touch) introduce children to entomology, botany, mammology, herpetology, geology, paleontology, and ornithology. Another room at the Visitor

Pavilion has a tree, a cave, and a creekbed and contains examples (stuffed) of Central Texas snakes, amphibians, insects, and birds.

On the grounds of the Nature Center is a bird enclosure for about twenty owls, hawks, buzzards, and crows that have survived various misadventures. Most of these crippling injuries have resulted from unhappy dealings with humans. The caged birds seem content enough in their safe harbors and are obviously treated kindly. Some of them respond to soothing words by tilting their heads, as if they have become accustomed to that tone of voice.

The sixty-acre **Zilker Nature Preserve** is adjacent to the grounds of the Austin Nature Center. In fact, the trailhead for the 2 miles of crisscrossing trails is at one end of the bird enclosure. The trails lead beside and across a seasonal creek with a steep limestone cliff, through a native grass meadow, and, if you can make the climb, up the side of a hill to a pavilion overlooking Austin. Until you crest the hill, you almost forget that you are only a few minutes from downtown Austin.

The Austin Nature Center and the Zilker Nature Preserve are located on the northwest side of Zilker Park and are reached by going west on Barton Springs Road and veering right on Stratford Drive. Signs direct you to the parking areas near the entrance to the Nature Center, which is virtually underneath Mopac (Loop 1).

The Nature Center is open Monday through Saturday, 9 A.M. to 5 P.M. and Sunday, 12 noon to 5 P.M. Informal nature presentations by volunteers are on Saturdays between 11 A.M. and 3 P.M. The mailing address is 301 Nature Center Drive, Austin, Texas 78746. Call (512) 327-8181. The Zilker Nature Preserve is open from dawn to dusk. No pets or bicycles are allowed. Free.

If, however, you want to take your dog for a walk or go on a bicycle ride, Austin has the goods. More than 25 miles of **hike and bike trails** have been developed in Austin since 1976, when a citywide greenbelt trail system was proposed. The Big Mama is the 10-mile trail around Town Lake, but shorter trails follow along creeks and through parks. Austin Parks and Recreation Department also maintains 169 parks, including the Big Daddy—as in 350 acres, miniature train, outdoor theater, canoe rentals, garden center, and Barton Springs pool—**Zilker Park.**

The offices of the Austin Parks and Recreation Department have trail maps and park information. The main office is located at 200 South Lamar and is open Monday through Friday, 8 A.M. to 5 P.M. The phone number is (512) 499-6700. These hours won't do you any good if you are in Austin on a weekend; however, **Austin Visitor Center** at 201 East Second Street is open on Saturdays from 9 A.M. to 5 P.M. and on Sunday from 1 P.M. to 5 P.M. as well as weekdays. If you visit the office or call (512) 478-0098, they can help you out. And, they are real cheerful about it, too.

With the possible exception of FAO Schwarz in New York City, **Terra Toys** is the best toy store that ever was made. Open Monday through Saturday, 10 A.M. to 7 P.M. and Sunday from 12 noon to 6 P.M. They are located at 1708 South Congress, and their phone number is (512) 445-4489.

Gotta' make a run to the **Capitol** if you haven't been there in the last couple of years—there's a new girl in town. The original Texas Goddess of Liberty on top of the Capitol was allowed to retire to the halls of the Texas Memorial Museum in 1986. In her place is a new Goddess of Liberty. But the new statue was only the beginning.

Renovations of the outside of her pedestal were completed in 1993, and renovations of the inside of the main Capitol Building were completed in 1995. Replacing the Goddess of Liberty reminds me of the new chair that forces replacement of the old couch, that forces replacement of the old carpet, that forces repainting of the walls, that forces new drapes, etc.

The **Visitor Information Center** in the Capitol is open daily from 8 A.M. to 5 P.M. Free guided tours are conducted between 8:30 A.M. and 4:30 P.M. every day. In the evening, after almost everyone has gone home, is a nice, step-echoing time to visit the rotunda, which is open until 11 P.M. Call (512) 463-0063 for more information.

Austin is brimming with good restaurants, eateries, and silage sheds (places that feed you health food.) But for a good hamburger, good French fries, good pie, good coffee, good waitresses, and a good chance to see someone I know, I go to **Frisco's**. This good restaurant has been at the same spot on the southeast corner of Burnet Road and Koenig Lane since 1952. The adult menu has steaks, seafood, chicken, and sandwiches, including the famous Friscoburger. The

State Capitol

children's menu has hamburgers, grilled cheese sandwiches, "top chop't steakettes," fried shrimp and PB & Js. A leaner choice includes broiled chicken breast served with choice of two vegetables. Frisco's is open every day from 7 A.M. to 10 P.M. Visit them at 5819 Burnet Road, or call (512) 459-6279. $$

Other burger places in Austin are **Hudson's Grill,** 13376 Research ([512] 219-1902) and 8440 Burnet Road ([512] 458-5117); **Magnolia Cafe,** 2304 Lake Austin Boulevard ([512] 478-8645) and 1920 South Congress Avenue ([512] 445-0000); **The Filling Station,** 801 Barton Springs Road ([512] 477-1022). $$–$$$

CLOSING WORDS

I cannot finish this section on Austin, or this book, without telling about Tris Johnson and Northwest Park. Tris, his twin sister Chris, and I were in the same Sunday School and Training Union classes at Highland Park Baptist Church. We went to the same junior high school, and later, the same high school. Our homes were less than a mile apart in Allandale, a housing division in northwest Austin fit for Ozzie and Harriet. Like all the other kids growing up in Allandale, we spent a lot of time at Northwest Park, a neighborhood park with a playground and a swimming pool and a baseball diamond. It was, and still is, a peaceful, safe place with friendly shadows.

Tris was twenty years old when he got drafted. He was in the U.S. Marines. There was sniper fire. When Tris wrote to me from Vietnam, the only thing he asked for were snapshots of Northwest Park. When he came home, he told me those pictures kept him from losing his mind.

As Nanci Griffith sings, everyone needs a place to go when they close their eyes. Remembering this place should make a person feel peaceful and safe. I sincerely hope that I pointed you and your family in the right direction for finding such a place.

Appendix 1
Using Texas State Parks

TEXAS CONSERVATION PASSPORT

For $25 a year you can get free entry for you and your family (in one vehicle) to all state parks that have a per-vehicle daily entrance fee. One passport is required per adult for entry to Texas Wildlife Management Areas and not-fully-developed state parks that permit self-guided tours. One Passport is required per adult to attend special tours and programs guided by experts in ecology, wildlife biology, archeology, and related fields. Children under twelve can go along with an adult Passport holder. Passport holders receive a calendar of Texas Conservation Passport activities every three months. Passport holders also receive a discount on *Texas Parks and Wildlife* magazine.

To apply, send your name, address, city, state, zip code, driver's license number with state identified, and date of application for your Passport to: Texas Conservation Passport, Texas Parks and Wildlife Department, 4200 Smith School Road, Austin, Texas 78744. Call (512) 389-4800 or (800) 792-1112 for more information.

CENTRAL RESERVATION CENTER

As of March 28, 1994, a centralized reservation system for the state park system has been in place. If you want to reserve a campsite or other facilities you can do so by calling the central number in Austin at (512) 389-8900. This is not a toll-free number. Two exceptions to the centralized system are the Texas State Railroad at Palestine/Rusk ([800] 442-8951) and Indian Lodge at Davis Mountains State Park ([915] 426-3254).

If you make reservations at least one week before the park visit is planned and confirm it with a MasterCard or Visa credit card, a computer-printout confirmation is mailed to you. If you make reservations and mail a check to Texas Parks and Wildlife Department within five working days before the scheduled visit, and if there is enough time to do so, a confirmation is mailed to you. If the reservation is made less than five working days before the scheduled visit, you can (1) confirm the reservation with a credit card, (2) mail in a check, or (3) pay at the park when you arrive. In any case, no confirmation is mailed.

The mailing address is Texas Parks and Wildlife Department, Reservation Center, P.O. Box 17488, Austin, Texas 78760-7488.

Appendix 2
Hospitals in South Central Texas
(listed by county)

All those listed below have emergency departments.
An asterisk (*) by the hospital name indicates that it is a certified
trauma center.

Atascosa
Jourdanton: Tri-City Community Hospital, Highway 97 East,
(210) 769-3515

Bastrop
Smithville: Smithville Hospital Authority, 701 East 9th Street,
(512) 237-5105

Bexar
San Antonio:
*Baptist Medical Center, 111 Dallas Street, (210) 222-8431
*University Hospital, 4502 Medical Center Drive, (210) 616-4000
*Northeast Baptist, 8811 Village Drive, (210) 653-2330
*Southeast Baptist, 4214 East Southcross, (210) 337-6900
North Central Baptist, 520 Madison Oak, (210) 491-4000
Southwest General Hospital, 7400 Barlite, (210) 921-2000

Burnet
Burnet: Highland Lakes Medical Center, U.S. Highway 281 South,
(512) 756-6000

Caldwell
Luling: Edgar B. Davis Memorial Hospital, 130 Hays,
(210) 875-5643

Comal
New Braunfels: McKenna Memorial Hospital, 143 East Garza,
(210) 606-9111

DeWitt
Cuero: Cuero Community Hospital, Yoakum Highway,
(512) 275-6191

Frio
Pearsall: Frio Hospital, 320 Berry Ranch Road, (210) 334-3617

Gillespie
Fredericksburg: Hill Country Memorial Hospital, 1020 Kerrville
Highway, (210) 997-4353

Goliad
Goliad: Goliad County Hospital, 329 West Franklin Street,
(512) 645-8221

Gonzales
Gonzales: Memorial Hospital, 1110 Sarah Dewitt, (210) 672-7581

Guadalupe
Seguin: Guadalupe Valley Hospital, 1215 East Court Street, (210)
379-2411

Hays
San Marcos: *Central Texas Medical Center, 1301 Wonder World
Drive, (512) 353-8979

Karnes
Kenedy: Otto Kaiser Memorial Hospital, U.S. Highway 181
North, (210) 583-3401

Kerr
Kerrville: Sid Peterson Memorial Hospital, 710 Water Street, (210)
896-4200

Center Point: Starlite Village Hospital, Elm Pass Road,
(210) 634-2212

Lampasas
Lampasas: Rollins-Brook Hospital, 608 North Key Ave,
(512) 556-3682

Lavaca
Yoakum: Yoakum Community Hospital, 303 Hubbard,
(512) 293-2321

Llano
Llano: Llano Memorial Hospital, 200 West Ollie, (915) 247-5040

Medina
Hondo: Medina County Hospital, 3100 Avenue E,
(210) 426-5363

Travis
Austin:
*Brackenridge Hospital, 601 East 15th Street, (512) 476-6461
*HCA South Austin Medical Center, 901 West Ben White
Boulevard, (512) 447-2211
*St. David's Hospital, 919 East 32nd Street, (512) 476-7111

Uvalde
Uvalde: Uvalde Memorial Hospital, 1025 Garner Field Road,
(210) 278-6251

Williamson
Georgetown: Georgetown Hospital, 2000 Scenic Drive,
(512) 930-5338
Taylor: Johns Community Hospital, 305 Mallard, (512) 352-7611
Round Rock: Round Rock Hospital, 2400 Round Rock Avenue,
(512) 255-6066

Wilson

Floresville: Wilson Memorial Hospital, 1301 Hospital Boulevard,
 (210) 393-3122

SOURCE: 1991 TDH/AHA/THA Annual Survey of Hospitals. This information was derived from a report prepared by the Bureau of State Health Data and Policy Analysis, Texas Department of Health, December, 1992.

Bibliography

Appel, David, T. H. Filer, Jr., and R. Scott Cameron. *How To Identify and Manage Oak Wilt in Texas.* New Orleans: Southern Forest Experiment Station, United States Department of Agriculture Forest Service, 1990.

Baccus, John. Telephone interview with author. San Marcos, Texas, October 1, 1993.

Bedichek, Roy. *Adventures with a Texas Naturalist.* Garden City, N.Y.: Doubleday and Company, 1947.

Boyd, Bob. *The Texas Revolution: A Day-by-Day Account.* San Angelo: San Angelo Standard, 1986.

Boyd, Eva Jolene, and Kevin Stillman. "Ingram's Magnificent Murals." *Texas Highways,* July, 1990, pp. 32–33.

Caro, Robert A. *The Years of Lyndon Johnson: The Path to Power.* New York: Alfred A. Knopf, 1990.

Cisneros, Sandra. *Women Hollering Creek and Other Stories.* New York: Vintage Books, 1991.

Dooley, Kirk. *The Book of Texas Bests.* Dallas: Taylor Publishing Company, 1988.

Enquist, Marshall. *Wildflowers of the Texas Hill Country.* Austin: Lone Star Botanical, 1987.

Ezzell, Carol. "Cave Creatures." *Science News,* February 8, 1992, pp. 88–91.

Gould, Frank W. *Common Texas Grasses: An Illustrated Guide.* College Station: Texas A&M University Press, 1978.

Grimes, R. *Goliad: 130 Years After: Refugio and Guadalupe Victoria, March 1836–1986. Day-by-day in the Words of Men Who Were There.* Victoria: Victoria Advocate Publishing Company, 1966.

Groneman, Bill. *Alamo Defenders: A Genealogy. The People and Their Words.* Austin: Eakin Press, 1990.

Hodge, Larry D., and Earl Nottingham. "Yoakum's Got the Goods." *Texas Highways,* February, 1991, pp. 2–9.

Hunter, J. Marvin. *Old Camp Verde: The Home of the Camels.* Bandera, Tex.: J. Marvin Hunter, 1948.

Hurley, Rachel, and Pam Peeler. Interview with author. Pleasanton, Texas, May 28, 1993.

Kelton, Elmer. *The Time It Never Rained.* Fort Worth: Texas Christian University Press, 1973.

Kingston, Mike, ed. *1994–1995 Texas Almanac.* Dallas: Dallas Morning News, 1993.

Little, Mickey. *Hiking and Backpacking Trails of Texas.* 3rd ed. Houston: Gulf Publishing Company, 1990.

Miller, L. A. "Arctiid Moth Clicks Can Degrade the Accuracy of Range Difference Discrimination in Echolocating Big Brown Bats, *Eptesicus fuscus.*" *Journal of Comparative Physiology,* May, 1991, pp. 571–79.

McComb, David G. *Texas: A Modern History.* Austin: University of Texas Press, 1989.

McDonald, Archie P., ed. *The Texas Experience.* College Station: Texas A&M University Press, 1986.

Parent, Laurence. *The Hiker's Guide to Texas.* Billings, Mont.: Falcon Press, 1992.

Peterson, Roger Tory. *A Field Guide to the Birds of Texas and Adjacent States.* Boston: Houghton Mifflin Company, 1988.

Pryor, Cactus. *Cactus Pryor Inside Texas.* Bryan, Tex.: Shoal Creek Publishers, 1982.

Roach, Joyce Gibson. *This Place of Memory: A Texas Perspective.* Denton: University of North Texas Press, 1992.

Roemer, Ferdinand von. *Texas, with Particular Reference to German Immigration and the Physical Appearance of the Country, Described through Personal Observation.* Translated by Oswald Mueller. San Antonio: Standard Printing Company, 1935.

Ruff, Ann. *Texas Water Recreation: A Roadrunner Guide.* Dallas: Taylor Publishing Company, 1990.

Schmidly, David J. *The Bats of Texas.* College Station: Texas A&M University Press, 1991.

Spearing, Darwin. *Roadside Geology of Texas.* Missoula, Montana: Mountain Press Publishing Company, 1991.

Steely, James Wright, and Joseph R. Monticone. *The Civilian*

Conservation Corps in Texas State Parks. Texas Parks and Wildlife Department, PWD BKK-4000-442A, August, 1986.

Syers, Ed. *Off the Beaten Trail.* Ingram, Tex.: OBT Press, 1965.

————. *Backroads of Texas.* 2nd ed. Houston: Gulf Publishing Company, 1988.

Tuttle, Merlin D. *America's Neighborhood Bats.* Austin: University of Texas Press, 1988.

Van Allsburg, Chris. *Just A Dream.* Boston: Houghton Mifflin Company, 1990.

Warnock, Barton, and Peter Koch. *Wildflowers of the Big Bend Country, Texas.* Alpine, Tex.: Sul Ross University, 1970.

Wasowski, Sally, and Julie Ryan. *Landscaping with Native Texas Plants.* Dallas: Texas Monthly Press, 1985.

Winsett, Marvin Davis. "Call Out Their Names Again." *Remembered Earth: A Book of Poems.* San Antonio: Naylor Company, 1962.

Yarbrough, C. L. *Canyon of the Eagles: A History of Lake Buchanan and Official Guide to the Vanishing Texas River Cruise.* Dallas: Taylor Publishing Company, 1989.

Index

Bauer's Antique Toy Museum
  (Fredericksburg), **42, 45**
Bedichek, Roy, 37–38, 54
Bee Cave, 57
Bergner, Hans, 43
best road, 109–10
bicycling: hike and bike trails (Aus-
  tin), 144; McKinney Falls State
  Park, 140
birds: at Austin Nature Center, 143–
  44; at Bastrop State Park, 13; at
  Cibolo Wilderness Trail, 22; at
  Enchanted Rock, 68; flightless, at
  Y. O. Ranch, 73; at Lake
  Buchanan, 26; at Lost Maples
  State Natural Area, 104–106; at
  Palmetto State Park, 82; at
  Pedernales Falls State Park, 63. *See
  also* bald eagles
Blanco: Blanco State Park and, 99,
  101; dinosaur tracks at, 101
Blue Hole Recreation Club, 111–14,
  113
Bluffton, 27–28
Boerne, sites near: Boerne City Park,
  22–23; Cave without a Name, 17–
  21, **19**; Cibolo Nature Center, 22–
  23; Cibolo Wilderness Trail, **20**,
  22–23; Country Spirit Restaurant,
  23
Bonham, James Butler, 47, 126–27
bookstores: Alamo, 128; Main Book
  Shop, 45; Visitor Center, Lyndon
  B. Johnson State Park, 95
botanical gardens: San Antonio
  Botanical Garden, 129–30; Zilker
  Park, 138
Bowie, James, 47, 127
brewery, 123
Buchanan, Lake, 24–28, **29**

Buescher State Park, 14
Buffalo Hump, 41
Bulverde, 134
Burnet, sites near: Hill Country Flyer,
  30, **31**; Inks Lake State Park, 30–
  31; Longhorn Cavern State Park,
  32; Riverwalk Cafe, 29; Suzie Q,
  28; Topline Gem and Minerals,
  29; Vanishing Texas River Cruise,
  24–28, **29**

Cain City, 35
camel experiment, 76
Camp Verde, **75**, 76–77
camping: Bastrop State Park, 13–14;
  Blanco State Park, 101; Blue Hole
  Recreation Club, 114; Buescher
  State Park, 14; Enchanted Rock
  State Natural Area, 69; Guadalupe
  River State Park, 134; Inks Lake
  State Park, 30–31; Kerrville-
  Schreiner State Park, 77; Lost
  Maples State Natural Area, 104;
  McKinney Falls State Park, 141;
  Palmetto State Park, 82; Pedernales
  Falls State Park, 63. *See also*
  summer camps
Capitol, 66, 138, 145, **146**
Carpenter, Liz, 127
cattle, 74, 98, 117–18
cattle brands, 118–19
caverns: Cave without a Name, 17–
  21, **19**, 71; Longhorn Cavern State
  Park, 32
Cave without a Name, 17–21, **19**, 71
cemetery, 123
Chisholm Trail, 117
Christmas Tree Forest (Yoakum),
  119–20, **121**
Cibolo Wilderness Trail (Boerne), **20**,

42, 45; Terra Toys, 145
train: Hill Country Flyer, 28, 30, 31;
    miniature train, 144
Travis, William B., 47, 87, 127
trees: bald cypress, 22, 58, 60–61, 60;
    blackbrush acacia, 93, 94; canyon
    maples, 102–104; eastern redbud,
    105; loblolly pines, 9, 13, 80; mes-
    quite, 53; Mexican buckeye, 63;
    oak decline, 7; sycamore, 53, 63,
    104–105, 130; Texas mountain
    laurel, 63, 105, 107
tunnel, 35
Tuttle, Merlin, 33, 37

Urrea, Jose, 49

Van Allsburg, Chris, 138
Vanderpool, sites near: Las Campanas,
    107, 109; Lost Maples State Natu-
    ral Area, 102–109, 105
Vanishing Texas River Cruise, 24–28,
    29
Van Zandt, Townes, 64
Vereins Kirche, 43, 44
vernal pools, 66
Vietnam, 135, 136–37, 147
Vietnam Veterans Memorial, 135, 137
von Roemer, Ferdinand, 32

wading: Blue Hole Recreation Club,
    111–14, 113; Guadalupe River
    State Park, 134; Hamilton Pool,
    57, 58; Inks Lake State Park, 30;

Lost Maples State Natural Area,
    106; McKinney Falls State Park,
    138–40, 142
Warm Springs Rehabilitation
    Hospital, 84–85
Warnock, Barton, 5
wasps, 136
Watermelon Thump, 86
Welfare, 37
Welhausen, Philip, 117
Westcave Preserve, 55, 58–61, 60
wildflowers, 54, 70, 92–93
Willow City Loop, 70–71
Wimberley, sites near: Blue Hole Rec-
    reation Club, 111–14, 113; Devil's
    Backbone, 116; Mount Alberta
    (Old Baldy), 114–15; shopping,
    116; Woolsey's Ice Cream Parlor
    and Deli, 116
Winsett, Marvin Davis, 127

Ximines, Damacio, 121

Y. O. Ranch, 72–76, 79
Yarbrough, C. L., 27–28
Yoakum, B. F., 117
Yoakum, sites in: Annual Christmas
    Tree Forest, 119–20, 121; Leather
    Capital Store, 118; Wieting's
    Steakhouse, 120; Yoakum Heritage
    Museum, 118–20, 121

Zilker Nature Preserve, 144
Zilker Park, 138, 144